About The Author

Lou Seibert Pappas is the food editor of the Peninsula Times Tribune in Palo Alto, California. A former food consultant for "Sunset Magazine," she now writes for "Gourmet" and "Cuisine" magazines and is the author of a dozen other cookbooks, including **Creative Soups and Salads, Extra-Special Crockery Pot Recipes and Bread Baking.** She has made 10 extensive trips to Europe collecting recipes and ideas for her books and taking photographs. She and her husband Nicholas, an electronics consultant, have four children: three sons and a daughter.

To Derek, Alexis, Christian and Niko—
Our quartet of cookie lovers.

COOKIES . . . FAVORITE TREATS FOR ALL SEASONS

- Over 100 recipes for a variety of tastes and occasions.

- Symbols clearly indicate which recipes make use of modern kitchen appliances, including the food processor and microwave oven.

- Special preparation, baking and storing tips are included so you will produce the best cookies ever, everytime.

- Contains all the recipes you need to bake old favorites, like Chocolate Chip, or something more exotic, like Cinnamon Apple Drops or Coconut Date Fingers.

- For easy use, the book lies flat when opened and is printed in large easy-to-read type.

- Compact design—takes a minimum of counter space.

Cookies

by Lou Seibert Pappas

Illustrated by Dorothy Cutright Davis

A Nitty Gritty Book*
Published by
Nitty Gritty Productions
P.O. Box 5457
Concord, California 94524

*Nitty Gritty Books-Trademark
Owned by Nitty Gritty Productions
Concord, California

Printed in the U.S.A.
by Mariposa Press
Concord, California
Edited by Maureen Reynolds

ISBN 0-911954-57-0
Library of Congress Catalog Card Number: 80-81247

4th Printing

Table of Contents

Introduction

From simple to sublime, cookies command a joyous following. The art of baking cookies goes back centuries. The wealth of international cookies run the gamut of plain to fancy. The rewards are multi-fold. Taste buds are pleased with a kaleidoscope of flavors. And generations become closer as youngsters acquire the expertise of elders.

Recalling the cookies of my youth brings fond memories of a childhood brimming with filled cookie tins. Raisin Oatmeal cookies and Caramel Slices were waiting for after school snacks. Sugar Cut-Outs greeted every holiday. At Christmastime, mother always made Spritz, a recipe treasured by her Swedish forebearers. They were swirled into rings or wreaths and jeweled with homemade raspberry jelly. The doctor's wife unfailingly delivered a plateful of yuletide cookies. My favorite, among the dozen kinds she bestowed upon us, were the chunky Apricot Brazil Nut Chews. So laden with nuts and fruits were these moist morsels, that the caramel-flavored dough could barely hold them together.

Adulthood brought trips abroad and a whirlwind of continental cookies. I was lucky enough to have many fine European cooks share their recipes with me.

The Scandinavian countries were my first port of call. On the Stroget in Copenhagen, marzipan "kager" caught my eye. Danish Roof-Tops were one such almond confection. Almost pure marzipan, these triangular cookies are shaped like golden roofs, dripping with frosting icicles.

In Helsinki, at the handsome bakery chain of coffee houses called "Fazar," there were dozens of pretty cookies. Some were sheathed in fondant and chocolate and showered with chopped pistachios. Though they vied with the choicest of pastries for attention, they stood the match. In Oslo, after a smorebrod lunch of rippled slices of smoked salmon, caviar, lobster and white asparagus, it was off to the "Kakker brod" shop for sweets. That meant a bag of Krum Kager or cone-shaped wafers filled with soft ice cream, berries and chocolate shavings.

Heading south, our next stop was Holland. We were fortunate to be there during carnival and tulip time. Red flower leis bedecked the hoods of tooting cars. Bakery windows sparkled with fruit-glazed tortes and diminutive cookies. The candy-like Caramel cookies and Chocolate-Tipped Orange Sticks were my favorite finds in this lovely land.

In Germany, whimsical chocolate lady bugs, ranging in size from a penny to a football, filled each bakery window. Wedged between the fruit tarts and the Black Forest Cherry Cakes were fancy butter Cookies and the specialty: gingerbread. These spicy, soft cookies were cut into heart, star and wreath shapes. The coffee houses in Vienna offered equally delicious wares. Would it be cafe mit schlag and Vanilla Crescents, Chocolate Marzipan Wafers or Linzer Bars?

Patisseries excelled in colorful, carefree Venice. Pinoccate, the four-inch round almond paste macaroons, studded with golden pine nuts were a winner. Biscotti (Italian for "cookies") came in dozens of flavors. Toasted slices of the anise-flavored cookies called Ancini were addictive.

Zonar's cookies in Athens presented Koulourakia, an Easter shortbread, in a handful of shapes: rings, twists and knots. In France, napoleons and strawberry tarts beckoned first. On second glance, golden-edged Lemon and Almond Tile cookies came into play. The two-toned chocolate circles, half-moons and bars dipped into melted chocolate and pistachio nuts also looked delectable.

What follows is a combination of the marvelous recipes I have collected in Europe and time-tested favorites from my childhood.

Lou Seibert Pappas
Portola Valley, California

Historic Lore

The word cookie is an anglicization of the Dutch word "koekje," a diminutive cake that was put in a child's stocking at Christmastime. Small molded or shaped cakes can be traced back to antiquity. Cookies, by many names, have played a role in cuisines throughout the world. Originally, cookies had a symbolic meaning. They were baked for special occasions and were composed of rare and unusual ingredients.

The anise-scented Springerle date back to the midwinter pagan celebration called Julfest. During the festival, animals were sacrificed to the gods. Because the poor could not afford to butcher animals merely for sacrifice, they offered tokens of animal-shaped cookies. These cookies most often took the shape of a rearing steed. Interestingly, Springerle is derived from the German phrase "a vaulting horse." This was the sacred animal of Wotan, King of the Nordic gods.

Dutch Speckulaas cookie molds have always depicted scenes or events. The first molds recaptured biblical highlights, such as Adam and Eve standing next to the tree of knowledge. Later, confectioners began sculpting wooden planks into molds which reflected the events of their town. The word Speckulaas is derived from the word speclilum, which means mirror.

Shortbread has always been a traditional Christmas and New Year's treat in

Scotland. The rich butter cake descends from the oatmeal bannock served at pagan Yule celebrations. The round bannock was scored with a circle in the center with wedges surrounding it. This was meant to symbolize the sun and its rays. Because it was considered unlucky to cut the shortbread into portions, it was always broken into pieces by hand.

Greek Kourabiedes have been served at weddings and festivals for hundreds of years. At Christmastime, a clove is studded into each cookie to signify the spices brought by the Maggi to the Christ child.

Nuremberg, the city which made the religious Lebkuchen cookie famous, also became a renowned spice trading center. Until the middle ages, spices were considered rare and costly. Only wealthy people who lived in metropolitan areas used them with any regularity. One of the first leavening agents was powdered deer and hart antlers. The modern equivalent, ammonium carbonate, or baking powder, is used throughout the world today. Ginger and pepper used to be used interchangeably. This explains why so many ginger cookies have a "pepper" prefix, even though they lack that spice as an ingredient: Swedish Pepparkakor and German Pfeffernuesse.

Ingredients

A cookie may taste different than the recipe intends if even a slight variation in the ingredients is made. For example, substituting margarine for butter will result in a less rich tasting cookie. Using whole wheat flour instead of, or in addition to bleached or unbleached flour will yield a more "nutty" tasting and somewhat heavier cookie.

Many cooks enjoy altering ingredients in recipes to suit their own tastes and dietary needs. The following is a brief explanation of some of the major foods that go into cookie making. Once a knowledge of how these components affect the outcome of the cookie is gained, a tastier cookie can be produced.

Butter lends a superb flavor to cookies. If for health or economic reasons you find it necessary to reduce the amount of butter, substitute a high quality margarine. Try to use at least one-third to one-half of the amount of butter specified in the recipe.

Sweeteners, such as granulated sugar, brown sugar and powdered sugar add sweetness to a recipe and also aid the cookie in browning. Light brown sugar produces lighter colored cookies than does dark brown sugar, and is therefore more often used in cookie recipes. Whenever brown sugar is called for in a recipe, make sure to pack it firmly in a measuring cup. Use a metal or plastic cup meant to measure dry ingredients, **not** a glass cup, which is meant for measuring liquid ingredients. It makes a difference. Honey, yet another sweetener, lends a special flavor and moistness to cookies. But because it is a liquid, it cannot simply be substituted for sugar in a recipe.

Eggs give a framework and structure to cookies. They bind ingredients together. All the recipes in this cookbook are based upon using large eggs. Small, medium or extra-large eggs will change the texture of the cookies. Egg yolks add a golden color to cookies. When added to dough in their hard-cooked form, they produce a tender texture when baked. Egg whites are most often used in macaroon and meringue cookies. Here's an easy way to produce perfectly beaten egg whites: Remove the cold eggs from the refrigerator. While they are still very cold, separate them. Let the whites warm up to room temperature. Choose a bowl to beat them in. It should be ultra-clean and free of even miniscule amounts of oils or fats. Plastic bowls are not recommended because they tend to retain traces of grease even after they have been washed in hot water. Copper, stainless-steel and glass are the best bowls to use. If chocolate or cocoa is incorporated into egg whites, fold it gently in after the whites have been beaten until stiff. Both of these types of chocolate contain fat.

Flour, all-purpose/bleached is traditionally used in cookie baking. However, unbleached flour may be used in its place. Do not use cake flour, unless it is specifically asked for. Add extra nutrition to cookies by substituting whole wheat flour for half of the all-purpose flour. Although the cookies will be heavier in texture, they will have a pleasant "nutty" flavor.

Chocolate, such as unsweetened, semi-sweet and cocoa, lend richness and flavor to cookies. Because chocolate scorches easily, caution should be used when it is melted. Place it in the top of a double boiler over hot water. Put pan over medium-high heat. Watch carefully while chocolate melts, stirring occasionally. If a recipe you are making calls for semi-sweet chocolate and all you have are chocolate chips, here's a guide to use: 1 cup of chocolate chips equals 6 ounces of semi-sweet chocolate in bar form; 2/3 cup chips equals 4 ounces of bar chocolate and 1/3 cup chips equals 2 ounces bar chocolate.

Nuts boost cookies with flavor and texture. Because nuts vary in density and weight, grinding them finely in a blender or food processor will take varying amounts of time. "Soft" nuts, such as walnuts and pecans will take less time to grind than will "hard" nuts such as filberts, almonds and Brazil nuts. If you use a food processor to grind your nuts it's wise to add a few tablespoons of sugar or flour called for in the recipe to the work bowl before you begin grinding.

Before You Bake:

- Choose sturdy, clean **cookie sheets** that are the right size for your oven. They should have at least two inches of airspace on all sides. This will allow the hot air to circulate around the dough, producing more evenly baked cookies. Avoid using dark-bottomed cookie sheets. They absorb too much heat and may cause your cookies to brown too quickly underneath. Also, baking sheets should not have high sides. These cause the heat to be deflected, producing unevenly baked cookies.

- If the cookie dough contains **a high proportion of butter or margarine,** greasing the baking sheets is unnecessary. If you are unsure, grease the sheets lightly. The **baking sheets should be cold** when you are arranging cookie dough on them, otherwise the dough may spread.

- It is best to **fill a cookie sheet evenly** with drops of dough. As a general rule, place drops of dough two inches apart, unless otherwise specified.

- Always use a **preheated oven.** Set your oven to the temperature the recipe directs before you begin preparing the cookies.

Baking Tips

- It's best to bake one sheet of cookies at a time. Place the sheet on the center rack of your oven. Check the cookies 5 minutes before the end of the specified baking time. Many factors affect the length of baking time: temperature of the day, humidity, handling of dough, how well the recipe was followed, if any substitutions in the recipes were made, your oven and how many sheets of cookies were baked at the same time.
- Let baking sheets cool before adding more dough to them.
- It's not necessary to grease the sheets between each batch of cookies. Simply remove the crumbs by wiping them with a paper towel.
- Remove the cookies from the baking sheets as soon as they are firm enough (usually 1 minute after baking). If the cookies should harden and stick to the sheet, return the cookies to the oven for a minute or two. This will soften the cookies a bit and allow you to remove them from the sheet.
- Bar cookies should be allowed to cool for about 10 to 15 minutes before they are cut into squares. To remove them easily from their pan, use a spatula.

Storing Tips

Proper storing is essential for cookies to remain in peak condition.
- Let freshly baked cookies cool to room temperature before sealing them in cans, otherwise they will soften.
- Store crisp cookies in containers with loose fitting lids. This will keep them crisp.
- Store soft cookies in containers with tight fitting lids. To help them retain their softness, place a small slice of apple in the container with the cookies.

Key To Symbols

When you see the following symbols, you'll know at a glance some of the special features of that recipe:

This recipe can be made with the aid of a food processor (see page 15 for more details).

These cookies may be baked in a microwave oven (see page 17 for more details).

These cookies may be frozen (see page 18 for more details).

This cookie travels well (see page 18 for more details).

This cookie has spices in it. 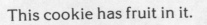   This cookie has chocolate in it.

This cookie has fruit in it.   This cookie has nuts in it.

Food Processor Hints

The food processor permits ultra-fast mixing, but timing is essential. Follow these guidelines when preparing cookie dough in your processor and avoid the common problem of overprocessing.

1. When creaming butter and sugar together, it's best to use chilled butter that has been cut into 1-inch cubes. Place the metal blade in the bowl. Add the butter and sugar and process until a ball of dough forms. Continue processing until the ball of dough dissolves and the mixture becomes soft and creamy.

2. If eggs are added to the dough, they will blend in about 3 seconds.

3. Dry ingredients will blend into creamed mixtures in about 5 to 8 seconds, depending upon the consistency of the dough.

4. If a recipe calls for shredded or chopped fruit or vegetables, do this before creaming the butter and sugar. Use the shredder attachment or the metal blade. Remove fruits or vegetables from the bowl and proceed with creaming. There's no need to wash or rinse bowl. When the recipe directs you to add the fruits or vegetables, you may let them chop into the dough, or stir them in by hand. The latter method is preferred because the fruits and vegetable tend to overchop if allowed to blend into the dough while the blade is in place.

5. Ground nuts should also be processed before you begin creaming the butter and sugar. Use the metal blade or the julienne disc. Be careful not to overprocess the nuts or they will become an oily mass, rather than a light and fluffy powder. Soft nuts, such as pecans, cashews and walnuts, process more quickly than do hard nuts, such as almonds and filberts. Allow about 5 seconds to process 1-1/2 cups of pecans; 15 seconds to process 1-1/2 cups almonds. Add a tablespoon or two of flour or sugar called for in the recipe to the nuts before grinding them. This will help them remain light and fluffy.

6. If a recipe calls for chopped soft nuts, such as walnuts or pecans, they may be added whole to the batter and allowed to chop as they blend. Harder nuts should be chopped with the metal blade before creaming the butter and sugar.

7. To avoid scratching the metal blade and the work bowl, use plastic or wooden utensils to remove the dough from the processor.

Microwave Adaptation

Certain types of cookies are better suited to the microwave oven than others. The best choices are stiff, crumbly batters with more flour in proportion to butter. Molded cookies work well, especially those meant to remain pale in color.

A sheet of cookies may take longer to bake in a microwave oven than in a conventional oven. Additionally, their texture may be different from conventionally baked cookies. Meringue drops become crisper and harder when microwave cooked.

Bar cookies adapt well to the microwave. However, they bake best in round baking dishes. Square baking dishes receive too much heat in their corners. If you use a square pan, protect the corners of the cookies by placing a strip of aluminum foil diagonally across the corners of the pan. Also, bar cookies should be rotated at least twice while they are baking. If the batter is especially dense, like brownie batter, the pan should be rotated more often. To convert a bar cookie which takes 15 to 20 minutes to bake in a 350°F. conventional oven, microwave at high for 2-1/2 to 7 minutes, rotating the pan one quarter turn, twice.

How To Freeze Cookies

Although many cookbooks suggest you may freeze cookies for as long as 1 year, a month, two at the most, is more realistic. After two or three months in the freezer, cookies just don't taste like they should, no matter how well they were packaged.

Choose unfrosted and sturdy, rather than fragile cookies. Wrap them in foil or plastic bags and place them in metal tins or plastic containers, anything that will prevent them from getting crushed in the freezer.

Frozen cookies take only about 10 minutes to defrost. To freshen slightly stale or soggy cookies, place them on a lightly greased cookie sheet. Put them in a 300°F. oven for about 5 or 10 minutes.

How To Ship Cookies

Choose unfrosted, sturdy cookies to ship. Those with nuts and dried fruits tend to travel the best.

To mail cookies out of town, it's best to wrap them individually in foil, waxed paper or plastic wrap. However, this is not a necessity. Next, choose a pretty tin or box you wish to place the cookies in. It should be sturdy. Line the box or tin with "bubbled" polyethylene paper, thick cardboard, popped corn or packing pieces. Place a thick piece of cardboard on the bottom of the box too. Cookies should be placed one layer at a time in the box or tin. Separate the layers with pieces of cardboard and fill the crannies with popped corn or packing pieces. Pack the entire box as tightly as possible without damaging the cookies. This will prevent them from moving and possibly breaking while they travel. The box or tin should now be placed in a larger box which has been filled with popped corn or packing pieces, sealed and shipped.

19

Drop Cookies

The dough for these cookies is soft enough to drop from a spoon into mounds on your baking sheet. A slender spatula makes a handy tool for pushing the dough from the spoon. When you flatten cookies before putting them into the oven, you'll get better results if, instead of using the traditional flat side of a knife or glass bottom dipped in water, you wet your fingers and use them to flatten the dough. The dough won't stick to your fingers as it sometimes does to the knife or glass.

If dropping the cookie dough onto the baking sheets seems tedious, enlist children for the task. All ages enjoy the challenge. And, extra hands transform the project into a fun family activity. Children will soon gain an appreciation for the diligence required in cookie baking. And they receive ample compensation as the cookies appear fresh-baked from the oven.

Sometimes it's fun to turn drop cookies into oversized rounds, like saucer-sized granola cartwheels, or giant chocolate chop "frisbees." These elicit especially resounding approval when tucked in a brown bag lunch or stacked on a platter at a party.

The Ultimate Chocolate Chunk Cookies

Chop the candy bar by hand. Don't use a food processor. It won't give uniformly-sized chunks.

1/2 cup unsalted butter,
  at room temperature
1 cup firmly packed brown sugar
1 egg
1/2 tsp. vanilla
1-1/8 cups all-purpose flour

1/2 tsp. baking soda
1/4 tsp. salt
6 ounce bar bittersweet chocolate
  (such as Lindt)
1/2 cup chopped filberts or pecans

Beat butter and sugar together until creamy. Beat in egg and vanilla. In a separate bowl, stir together flour, soda and salt. Add to creamed mixture. Beat well. Chop chocolate into approximately 1/4-inch chunks. By hand, stir in chocolate and nuts. Drop by rounded teaspoonfuls onto greased baking sheets. Bake in a 375°F. oven for 8 minutes, or until golden brown. Immediately remove to wire racks to cool. Makes about 6 dozen.

Hints: If desired, substitute 1/2 cup whole wheat flour for 1/2 cup all-purpose flour. Try using milk chocolate instead of bittersweet chocolate too.

Oatmeal Chocolate Chippers

Very good
1/2000
Wedgwood

1 cup butter or margarine, at room temperature
3/4 cup EACH granulated sugar and firmly packed brown sugar
2 eggs
1 tsp. vanilla
3/4 cup EACH all-purpose flour and whole wheat flour
1 tsp. baking soda
1/2 tsp. salt
2 cups quick cooking rolled oats
1 cup chopped walnuts or pecans
1 large package (12 ozs.) chocolate chips

23

Beat butter and sugars together until creamy. Beat in eggs and vanilla. In a separate bowl, stir together flours, soda and salt. Add to creamed mixture. Beat well. By hand, stir in oats, nuts and chips. Drop by rounded teaspoonfuls onto greased baking sheets. Bake in a 350°F. oven for 10 to 12 minutes, or until golden brown. Remove to wire racks to cool. Makes about 6 dozen.

Hint: If using food processor, stir oats, nuts and chocolate chips in by hand.

Granola Crunchies

Either raisins or chocolate chips can embellish these up-dated drop cookies that were once popularly known as Ranger Cookies.

1 cup butter, at room temperature
1 cup EACH granulated sugar and firmly packed brown sugar
2 eggs
1 tsp. vanilla
2 cups all-purpose flour
1 tsp. baking soda
1/2 tsp. EACH baking powder and salt
2 cups granola
1-1/2 cups slightly crushed wheat flakes
1/3 cup wheat germ OR bran flakes
1 cup raisins OR chocolate chips
1 cup chopped walnuts OR
    coarsely chopped toasted almonds

24

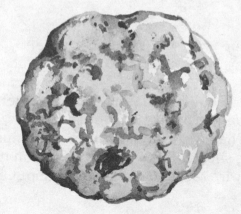

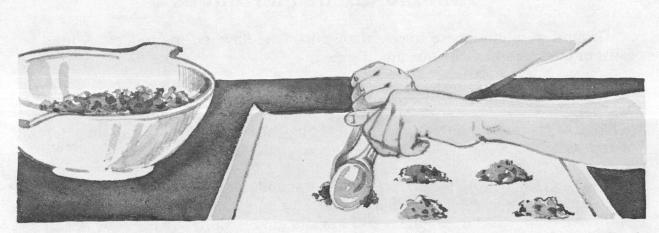

25

Beat butter and sugars together until light and creamy. Beat in eggs and vanilla. In a separate bowl, stir together flour, soda, baking powder and salt. Add to creamed mixture. Beat well. By hand, stir in granola, wheat flakes, wheat germ, raisins and nuts. Mix until thoroughly combined. Drop by rounded teaspoonfuls onto greased baking sheets. Flatten slightly with a fork. Bake in a 350°F. oven for 10 to 15 minutes, or until golden brown. Remove immediately to wire racks to cool. Makes about 6 dozen.

Hint: If using food processor, stir granola, wheat flakes, wheat germ, raisins and nuts in by hand.

Almond Cocoa Meringues

Ground nuts punctuate these crispy chocolate-flavored meringues. A food processor or blender will make the grinding easy.

3 egg whites, at room temperature
1 tsp. vanilla
1/8 tsp. EACH cream of tartar and salt
3/4 cup sugar

1/3 cup unsweetened cocoa
3/4 cup ground almonds or filberts
blanched almond halves (about 3 dozen)

Beat egg whites with vanilla, cream of tartar and salt until soft peaks form. Reserve 2 tablespoons sugar. Beat remaining sugar into egg whites, 1 tablespoon at a time. Continue beating until meringue is stiff but still glossy. Combine the reserved 2 tablespoons sugar with cocoa and fold in gently. Fold in ground nuts. Drop by tablespoonfuls (or use a pastry bag fitted with a star tip) onto baking sheets that are lined with foil or baking parchment. Place an almond half on top of each. Place in a 350°F. oven. Immediately turn off oven and let bake dry for 2 hours, or until firm. Remove from pans and store in an air-tight container. Makes about 3 dozen.

Chocolate Almond Macaroons

Shredded chocolate enhances these traditional nut macaroons.

3/4 cup almonds or filberts
3 ozs. semi-sweet chocolate OR 1/2 cup chocolate chips
3 egg whites, at room temperature
1/8 tsp. salt
3/4 cup sugar
1/2 tsp. vanilla

Using a food processor or blender, separately grind nuts and chocolate finely. Remove from appliance and set aside. Using an electric mixer or wire whip, beat egg whites until foamy. Add salt and beat until soft peaks form. Gradually beat in sugar, beating until stiff and glossy. Fold in nuts, chocolate and vanilla. Drop by rounded teaspoonfuls onto lightly greased baking sheets. Bake in a 300°F. oven for 20 minutes, or until lightly browned but still moist in the center. Remove immediately to wire racks to cool. Makes about 3 dozen.

Spicy Walnut Meringues

A hint about separating eggs: They are easiest to separate when they are cold, right from the refrigerator. However, the whites whip best and result is more volume when they are at room temperature, about 70°F.

2 cups (8 ozs.) walnuts
3 egg whites, at room temperature
1/8 tsp. salt
2/3 cup firmly packed brown sugar

1 tsp. vanilla
3/4 tsp. cinnamon
1/2 cup granulated sugar

Using a food processor or blender grind the nuts finely. Beat egg whites until foamy. Add salt and beat until soft peaks form. Add brown sugar, 1 tablespoon at a time, and beat until meringue is stiff. Beat in vanilla and cinnamon. Fold in ground nut meats. Drop meringue by teaspoonfuls into granulated sugar which has been spread out on waxed paper and roll until meringue is sugar coated. Place on greased baking sheets. Bake in a 325°F. oven for 12 to 15 minutes, or until golden brown. Makes 2-1/2 dozen.

Hint: To avoid overprocessing the nuts, grind them with 2 tablespoons brown sugar. Grind the nuts in small batches to keep nuts light and fluffy.

Coconut Cream Jumbles

Coconut laces together these tender sour cream drops. They are more like little cupcakes than cookies.

2 eggs
1-1/2 cups sugar
1 cup sour cream
1 tsp. vanilla
2 cups shredded coconut

3 cups cake flour
3 tsp. baking powder
1/2 tsp. baking soda
1/4 tsp. salt

29

Beat eggs until light and fluffy. Beat in sugar. Add sour cream, vanilla and coconut. Mix well. Sift flour, measure and sift again with baking powder, soda and salt. Stir into sour cream mixture. Cover and chill 1 hour. Drop by rounded teaspoonfuls onto greased baking sheets. Bake in a 400°F. oven for 12 to 15 minutes, or until golden brown around the edges. Makes 4 dozen cookies.

Niko's Peanut Butter Cookies

For variety, add 3/4 cup chopped peanuts or chocolate chips to the batter.

1/2 cup butter, at room temperature
1/2 cup peanut butter
1/2 cup EACH firmly packed brown sugar and granulated sugar
1 egg
1 tsp. vanilla
1-3/4 cups all-purpose flour
1 tsp. baking soda
1/2 tsp. salt

Beat butter, peanut butter and sugars together until creamy. Beat in egg and vanilla. In a separate bowl, stir together flour, soda and salt. Add to creamed mixture. Shape teaspoonfuls of dough into balls and place on greased baking sheets. Using a fork, mark each with a "X." Bake in a 375°F. oven for 10 to 12 minutes, or until golden brown. Remove to wire racks to cool. Makes 3 dozen.

Hint: To make Peanut Butter Blossoms, shape dough into 1-inch balls and roll in granulated sugar. Bake as directed above but don't flatten balls. When done press a Hershey's milk chocolate "Kiss" into the center of each cookie. Set aside to cool for an hour or two before storing.

Raisin Oatmeal Cookies

For variety, let candied orange peel replace the raisins.

1/2 cup raisins
1/2 cup butter, at room temperature
1/2 cup firmly packed brown sugar
1/4 cup granulated sugar
2 eggs
1 tsp. vanilla
1 cup all-purpose flour

3/4 cup rolled oats
1/2 tsp. baking soda
1/2 tsp. salt
2 tsp. grated orange peel
1/2 cup wheat germ
1/3 cup finely chopped
  walnuts or pecans

Finely chop raisins with a knife or a food processor. If using a processor, remove after chopped and set aside. Beat butter and sugar together until creamy. Beat in eggs and vanilla. In separate bowl, stir together flour, oats, soda, salt, and orange peel. Add to creamed mixture. Stir in wheat germ, nuts and raisins. Refrigerate for 30 minutes. Drop rounded teaspoonfuls of dough onto greased baking sheets, 3 inches apart. Bake in a 350°F. oven for 10 minutes, or until golden brown. Remove immediately to wire racks to cool. Makes 2-1/2 dozen cookies.

Hint: If using food processor, let whole nuts chop into batter as they blend, OR stir them in already chopped by hand.

Orange Walnut Cookies

Orange juice concentrate highlights these crispy raisin drops. The whole wheat flour, non-fat dry milk powder and bran flakes add extra nutrition too.

3/4 cup butter or margarine,
   at room temperature
1-1/4 cups firmly packed brown sugar
1 egg
1/4 cup frozen orange
   juice concentrate, thawed
1 cup whole wheat flour

1/4 cup non fat dry milk powder
1/2 tsp. salt
1 tsp. baking powder
1/4 cup bran flakes or wheat germ
1-1/2 cups quick cooking rolled oats
1/2 cup raisins, chopped
1 cup finely chopped walnuts

Beat butter, sugar and egg together until fluffy. Add orange juice concentrate. Beat well. In separate bowl, stir together flour, milk powder, salt, baking powder and bran flakes. Add to creamed mixture, mixing well. Stir in oats, raisins and nuts. Drop by heaping teaspoonfuls onto lightly greased baking sheets. Flatten slightly with wet fingers. Lightly sprinkle with sugar. Bake in a 350°F. oven for 10 to 12 minutes, or until lightly browned. Remove to wire racks and let cool. Makes 4-1/2 dozen cookies.

Hint: If using a food processor, let oats, raisins and nuts chop into batter as they blend, OR stir them in by hand.

Cornflake Meringues

These should be baked until they have a golden look, but still retain a chewy moist center.

4 egg whites, at room temperature
1-1/4 cups sugar
dash salt
1 tsp. vanilla
1-1/2 cups cornflakes
1 cup chopped walnuts

34

In the top of a double boiler, beat egg whites with a portable electric mixer until soft peaks form. Gradually beat in sugar and salt. Place over simmering water and beat constantly for 7 minutes, or until stiff and glossy. Remove from heat and stir in corn flakes and nuts. Drop from tablespoonfuls onto greased baking sheets. Bake in a 325°F. oven for 5 to 8 minutes, or until light, golden brown. Makes about 4 dozen.

Hermits

It is claimed that these cookies originated during the days of the clipper ships. Because they keep well for up to 3 weeks, they endured the ship voyages.

They are also known as Rox.

2/3 cup butter or margarine, at room temperature
1-1/2 cups firmly packed brown sugar
2 eggs
2-1/2 cups all-purpose flour
1 tsp. EACH baking soda and cinnamon
1/4 tsp. EACH salt, cloves and allspice
3/4 cup EACH chopped walnuts or pecans AND raisins

Beat butter and sugar together until creamy. Beat in eggs. In a separate bowl, stir together flour, soda, cinnamon, salt, cloves and allspice. Add to creamed mixture, blending well. Mix in nuts and raisins. Drop by rounded teaspoonfuls onto greased baking sheets. Bake in a 375°F. oven for 8 to 10 minutes, or until golden brown. Remove immediately to wire racks to cool. Makes about 5 dozen.

Hint: If using a food processor, let whole nuts and raisins chop into batter as they blend. This will enhance the flavor of these cookies.

Sesame Seed Snaps

3/4 cup sesame seed
1/2 cup butter or margarine, at room temperature
1-1/2 cups firmly packed brown sugar
1 egg
3/4 cup all-purpose flour
1/2 tsp. baking powder
1/8 tsp. salt
1 tsp. vanilla

36

Sprinkle sesame seed in a shallow baking pan. Toast in a 350°F. oven for 10 to 12 minutes, or until lightly browned. Shake pan occasionally to brown seed evenly. Let cool. Beat butter and sugar together until smooth. Beat in egg. In separate bowl, stir together flour, baking powder and salt. Add to creamed mixture beating until smooth. Add vanilla and toasted sesame seed, mixing lightly. Drop dough by teaspoonfuls onto buttered baking sheets, leaving 2-1/2 inches of space between each cookie. Bake in a 325°F. oven for 8 minutes, or until lightly browned. Remove pan from oven and let cool 1 minute, then remove cookies to wire racks to cool. Makes 60 cookies.

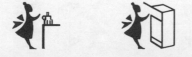

Healthy Breakfast Gems

These nutrition-packed cookies are a delight to toddlers and adults alike. Great for those "on-the-run" breakfast eaters.

1 egg
1/2 cup firmly packed brown sugar
1 tbs. vegetable oil
1/4 tsp. salt
1 tsp. vanilla
1/3 cup EACH rolled oats and bran flakes
2 tbs. wheat germ
1/2 cup EACH chopped pecans or walnuts AND golden raisins

Beat egg until light. Gradually add brown sugar, beating until light and fluffy. Add oil, salt, vanilla, oats, bran flakes, wheat germ, nuts and raisins. Mix well. Drop by rounded tablespoonfuls onto greased baking sheets. Bake in a 350°F. oven for 8 minutes, or until golden brown. Remove immediately from baking sheets and let cool on wire racks. Makes about 18 cookies.

Hints: If using a food processor, let whole nuts and raisins chop as they blend into batter or stir them in already chopped by hand.

Coconut Oatmeal Crisps

These caramelized oatmeal saucers were a childhood favorite—crackly big 5-inch cartwheels that seemed to last forever. This version is scaled down slightly for easier handling.

2 eggs
1 cup firmly packed brown sugar
2 cups rolled oats
1/2 cup vegetable oil
3 tbs. sesame seed
1/4 cup wheat germ

1/4 tsp. salt
1 tsp. vanilla
1 cup flaked coconut
1/2 cup finely chopped
   walnuts or pecans

Beat eggs with an electric mixer or wire whisk until light. Add sugar, oats, oil, seed, wheat germ, salt, vanilla and coconut. Mix well. Cover bowl and let stand 2 hours at room temperature. Mix in walnuts. Drop by rounded tablespoonfuls onto greased baking sheets 3 inches apart. Pat out thinly with a spatula, leaving 1 inch between cookies. Bake in a 350°F. oven for 8 to 10 minutes, or until lightly browned. Remove immediately to racks to cool. Store in air tight container. Makes 30 cookies.

Hint: DON'T make these with a food processor.

Cinnamon Apple Drops

This chewy cookie is packed full of healthy ingredients.

2/3 cup butter, at room temperature
1-1/4 cups firmly packed brown sugar
2 eggs
1/4 cup plain yogurt
1 cup EACH all-purpose flour
  and whole wheat flour
1 tsp. EACH baking powder and cinnamon

1/2 tsp. EACH salt, baking soda,
  and allspice
1-1/2 cups coarsely grated,
  peeled and seeded tart apple
1 cup raisins
3/4 cup chopped walnuts or pecans

39

Beat butter and sugar together until creamy. Beat in eggs and yogurt. In separate bowl, stir together flours, baking powder, cinnamon, salt, soda and allspice. Add to creamed mixture. By hand, stir in apples, raisins and nuts. Drop by tablespoonfuls onto lightly greased baking sheets. Bake in a 375°F. oven for 8 to 10 minutes, or until golden brown. Remove immediately to wire racks to cool. Makes 4 dozen.

Hints: If using food processor, shred peeled and seeded apple with shredder attachment first. Remove from bowl. Prepare dough.

Carrot Cookies

These nutritious cookies are perfect for brown baggers.

1/2 cup butter, at room temperature
1-1/2 cups firmly packed brown sugar
2 eggs
1-1/4 cups whole wheat flour
1/3 cup wheat germ
1/3 cup bran flakes

1/2 tsp. baking soda
1/2 tsp. salt
1 tsp. cinnamon
2 cups rolled oats
1 cup golden raisins OR chopped dates
1 cup shredded carrots

41

Beat butter and sugar together until creamy. Mix in eggs. In separate bowl, stir together flour, wheat germ, bran flakes, soda, salt and cinnamon. Add to creamed mixture. Mix well. By hand, stir in oats, raisins and carrots. Drop by rounded teaspoonfuls onto a greased baking sheet. Bake in a 350°F. oven for 10 to 12 minutes, or until golden brown. Remove to wire racks to cool. Makes 4 dozen.

Hints: If using processor, chop dates with wheat germ first. Remove steel blade and insert shredding attachment, leaving dates in bowl. Shred carrots right into dates. Remove from processor. Without cleaning bowl, proceed with creaming.

Chocolate Date Cookies

These soft chocolate cookies can be prepared in a variety of ways. They may be frosted or not, and chocolate chips may replace the dates.

1/2 cup butter, at room temperature
1 cup firmly packed brown sugar
2 squares (2 ozs.) unsweetened chocolate, melted
1 egg
1/3 cup milk
1-2/3 cups all-purpose flour
1 tsp. baking powder
1/4 tsp. baking soda
1/2 cup chopped walnuts, pecans OR filberts
1 cup chopped dates OR 6 ozs. chocolate chips
Chocolate Frosting, see next page (optional)

Beat butter and brown sugar together until creamy. Beat in melted chocolate and egg. Add milk. Mix well. In a separate bowl, stir together flour, baking powder and soda. Add to creamed mixture. Stir in nuts and dates. Drop by rounded teaspoonfuls onto greased baking sheets. Bake in a 375°F. oven for 8 to 10 minutes, or until set. Immediately remove to wire racks to cool. If desired, frost with Chocolate Frosting. Makes about 4-1/2 dozen cookies.

Chocolate Frosting

2 tbs. butter
2 ozs. unsweetened chocolate
2 cups powdered sugar
3 tbs. water

Melt butter and chocolate in top of double boiler over simmering, not boiling, water. Stir in powdered sugar. Add water enough to make frosting of spreading consistency.

Hint: If using food processor, let whole nuts and dates chop into batter as they blend OR stir them in (already chopped) by hand.

Zucchini Orange Rounds

Orange zest and juice concentrate enliven these zucchini cookies.

3/4 cup butter, at room temperature
1-1/2 cups sugar
1 egg
1 tsp. vanilla
1-1/2 cups shredded zucchini
2-1/2 cups all-purpose flour
2 tsp. baking powder

2 tsp. grated orange peel
1/2 tsp. salt
2 tbs. frozen orange juice concentrate,
   thawed and undiluted
3/4 cup flaked coconut
3/4 cup chopped almonds or walnuts

Beat butter and sugar together until creamy. Beat in egg, vanilla and zucchini. In a separate bowl, stir together flour, baking powder, orange peel and salt. Add to creamed mixture. Beat well. Add orange concentrate, coconut and nuts. Mix well. Drop by rounded teaspoonfuls onto greased baking sheets. Bake in a 375°F. oven for 8 to 10 minutes, or until lightly browned. Cool on wire racks. Makes about 4 dozen.

Hints: If using a food processor, shred zucchini first using shredder attachment. Remove from bowl. Prepare dough. Let coconut and nuts chop in at end, OR stir them in by hand.

Pumpkin Cookies

This favorite Halloween spice cookie can be made with a steamed and pureed jack-o-lantern instead of canned pumpkin.

3/4 cup firmly packed brown sugar
2 tbs. honey
1 cup canned pumpkin
1/2 cup vegetable oil
1 tsp. vanilla
2 cups all-purpose flour
1 tsp. EACH baking powder and soda

1/2 tsp. EACH salt, cinnamon
 and nutmeg
1/4 tsp. ginger
1 cup chopped pitted prunes
 or raisins
1/2 cup chopped walnuts

Place brown sugar, honey, pumpkin, oil, and vanilla in a mixing bowl. Beat until blended. In a separate bowl, stir together flour, baking powder, soda, salt, cinnamon, nutmeg, and ginger. Add dry ingredients to pumpkin mixture. Mix well. By hand, stir in prunes and nuts. Drop by rounded teaspoonfuls onto greased baking sheets. Bake in a 350°F. oven for 12 to 15 minutes, or until golden brown. Remove to wire racks to cool. Makes 3 dozen.

Hint: Process prunes and nuts with 2 tablespoons flour before mixing batter, OR add whole to prepared batter and let them chop as they blend into batter.

Caramel Date Drops

Sour cream enriches and softens these fruit and nut-filled cookies. For variety, omit the dates and nuts from the recipe. Instead, stuff 36 dates with a piece of walnut or pecan and cover each date with batter. Bake at 375°F. for 8 to 10 minutes.

1/4 cup butter or margarine, at room temperature
3/4 cup firmly packed brown sugar
1 egg
1/2 tsp. vanilla
1-1/4 cups all-purpose flour
1/2 tsp. baking soda
1/4 tsp. baking powder
1/4 tsp. salt
1/2 cup sour cream
24 pitted dates, chopped
1/3 cup chopped walnuts or pecans
Frosting, see next page

Cream butter, sugar and egg together until fluffy. Mix in vanilla. In separate bowl, stir together flour, soda, baking powder and salt. Add to creamed mixture alternately with sour cream. Stir in dates and nuts. Drop by a rounded teaspoonfuls onto greased baking sheets. Bake in a 400°F. oven for 10 minutes, or until golden brown. Remove immediately to wire racks and let cool. Spread with frosting. Makes about 3-1/2 dozen.

FROSTING

1/4 cup butter
1 cup powdered sugar
1/2 tsp. vanilla

Melt butter in a small saucepan over medium-low heat. Stir in powdered sugar and vanilla. Add a few drops of hot water until the frosting reaches the proper spreading consistency.

Hints: If using food processor, let whole dates and nuts chop into batter as they blend, OR stir them in (already chopped) by hand.

Persimmon Cookies

1 cup persimmon puree
1 tsp. baking soda
1/2 cup butter, at room temperature
1 cup sugar
1 egg
1 tsp. vanilla
2 cups whole wheat flour
1/2 tsp. baking powder
1 tsp. cinnamon
1/2 tsp. nutmeg
1/4 tsp. EACH cloves and salt
1 cup raisins
3/4 cup chopped walnuts or pecans

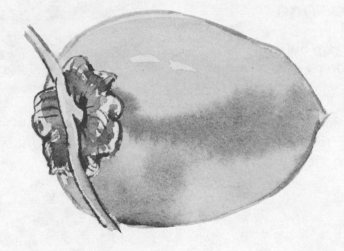

Combine persimmon puree and soda and let stand (it will thicken). Beat butter and sugar together until creamy. Beat in egg and vanilla. In separate bowl, stir together whole wheat flour, baking powder, cinnamon, nutmeg, cloves, and salt. Add to creamed mixture alternately with the persimmon puree. Stir in raisins and nuts. Drop by rounded teaspoonfuls onto a greased baking sheet. Bake in a 350°F. oven for 15 to 18 minutes, or until golden brown. Remove to wire racks to cool. Makes about 3 dozen.

Hints: Puree slices of peeled and seeded persimmon in food processor or blender. If using processor, there's no need to wash bowl, simply proceed with creaming. Let whole nuts and raisins chop into batter as they blend, OR stir them in (already chopped) by hand.

Snickerdoodles

Recipes for these crinkly cookies can be found in old-time church cookbooks under such names as Snipdoodles and Sneck Noodles. They are traditionally baked at Christmastime, but these cinnamon-sugar coated cookies are a treat year-round.

1/2 cup EACH butter and margarine,
  at room temperature
1-1/2 cups sugar
2 eggs
2-3/4 cups all-purpose flour
1-1/2 tsp. cream of tartar

1 tsp. baking soda
1/4 tsp. salt

Topping:
  3 tsp. sugar
  1 tsp. cinnamon

50

Beat butter, margarine and sugar together until creamy. Mix in eggs. In a separate bowl, stir together flour, cream of tartar, soda and salt. Add to creamed mixture. Mix well. Shape into balls about 1 inch in diameter. Chill 1 hour. Combine topping ingredients in small bowl. Drop dough balls into topping mixture. Coat well. Place on greased baking sheets about 2 inches apart. Bake in a 375°F. oven for 10 minutes, or until golden brown. Remove to wire racks and let cool. Makes 5 dozen cookies.

Sugar and Spice Cookies

These spicy cookies spread and crackle while baking.

3/4 cup butter, at room temperature
1 cup sugar
1 egg
1/4 cup molasses
2 cups all-purpose flour
2 tsp. baking soda

1/4 tsp. salt
1 tsp. cinnamon
3/4 tsp. cloves
3/4 tsp. ginger
powdered sugar

51

Beat butter and sugar together until creamy. Beat in egg and molasses. In a separate bowl, stir together flour, soda, salt, cinnamon, cloves and ginger. Add to creamed mixture. Mix well. Shape into balls, using rounded teaspoonfuls of dough. Place on a greased baking sheet. Bake in a 375°F. oven for 10 to 12 minutes, or until golden brown. Transfer to wire racks and let cool slightly. Dust with powdered sugar. Makes 4 dozen.

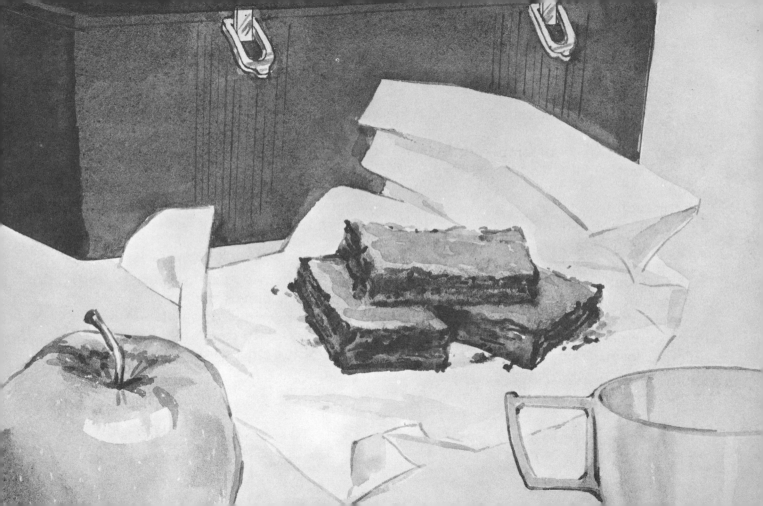

Bar Cookies

These are the easiest and quickest of all cookies to produce in a uniform size. After baking the bars it's wise to let them cool from 5 to 10 minutes before scoring them.

Because bar cookies are really a cross between a cake and a cookie, it's best to thoroughly grease or butter the pan they are to be baked in. If the bar is extremely fragile, dusting the buttered pan with flour is also a good idea.

It's important to use the size pan called for in each recipe. If you use a pan smaller than the one called for, you'll probably have much "cakier" cookies than were intended. A too large pan will result in dry and possibly crumbly bars.

Cookie bars are a choice traveler. For picnics, other outings or mailing, they can't be beat. If you are attending a buffet, potluck or picnic, tote the bars right in the pan in which they were baked. If you intend to mail them, they will travel best if individually wrapped in aluminum foil, cellophane or plastic wrap.

Rocky Road Bars

Marshmallows melt into a puffy sheen throughout these walnut-laced brownies.

2 ozs. unsweetened chocolate
1/2 cup butter
2 eggs
1 cup sugar
3/4 cup all-purpose flour

1/2 tsp. baking powder
1/4 tsp. salt
1/2 tsp. vanilla
1 cup miniature marshmallows
1 cup chopped walnuts or pecans

Melt chocolate and butter in the top of a double boiler over hot water. Let cool to room temperature. Using an electric mixer or wire whip beat eggs until thick and light. Gradually beat in sugar. Stir in melted chocolate mixture. In a separate bowl, stir together flour, baking powder and salt. Add to egg mixture. Beat well. Add vanilla, marshmallows and nuts. Turn into a greased 9-inch square pan. Bake in a 325°F. oven for 25 to 30 minutes, or just until barely set. Let cool, then cut into squares. Makes 3 dozen.

Christian's Chocolate Almond Bars

This favorite cookie is one that children can easily master.

1 cup butter, at room temperature
3/4 cup firmly packed brown sugar
2 cups all-purpose flour
1 tsp. vanilla extract
1 pkg. (6 ozs.) semi-sweet chocolate chips
3/4 cup finely chopped toasted almonds

55

    Place butter, sugar, flour and vanilla in a mixing bowl. Mix until crumbly. Pat into an ungreased 10 x 15-inch baking pan. Bake in a 350°F. oven for 15 to 20 minutes, or until golden brown. Remove from oven and sprinkle with chocolate chips. Let stand 1 minute until chocolate melts, then spread evenly. Sprinkle with nuts. Let cool, then cut into bars. Makes about 4-1/2 dozen.

Chocolate Mint Sticks

These ultra rich bars consist of three layers: the first is a brownie crust, the second a pale green mint center and the third chocolate frosting.

2 ozs. unsweetened chocolate
1/2 cup butter
2 eggs
1 cup sugar
1/2 cup all-purpose flour
1/2 cup sliced almonds

Peppermint Filling, see next page
Chocolate Frosting, see next page

56

In the top of a double boiler, melt chocolate and butter together over hot water. Remove from heat. Beat eggs and sugar together until light and fluffy. Stir the chocolate mixture, flour and nuts into the egg mixture. Beat well. Pour into a greased and floured 9-inch square baking pan. Bake in a 350°F. oven for 25 minutes, or until a toothpick inserted into the center comes out clean. Let cool on wire rack. Spread Peppermint Filling over the brownie layer. Cover and chill until firm. Drizzle Chocolate Frosting over filling. Cover and chill until set. Cut into strips. Makes about 3 dozen.

Peppermint Filling

1-1/2 cups sifted powdered sugar
3 tbs. soft butter
2 tbs. milk

1/2 tsp. peppermint extract
few drops green food coloring

Beat together all ingredients, except food coloring, until smooth. Add food coloring, a few drops at a time, until desired degree of "greeness" is reached.

Chocolate Frosting

2 ozs. semi-sweet chocolate
2 tbs. butter

In the top of a double boiler, melt chocolate and butter over hot water. Stir until smooth.

Fudge Brownies

Rich and chocolatey, these bars are best if not over-baked. Let them be still moist and soft inside.

4 squares (each 1 oz.) unsweetened chocolate
1 cup butter
4 eggs, at room temperature
2 cups sugar
2 tsp. vanilla

1 cup all-purpose flour
dash salt
1-1/2 cups chopped walnuts or pecans
powdered sugar (optional)

In the top of a double boiler, melt chocolate and butter over hot water. Let cool. Beat eggs until light with an electric beater or wire whip. Beat in sugar and vanilla. Stir in chocolate mixture. Mix in flour, salt and nuts. Turn into a greased and floured 9 x 13-inch baking pan. Bake in a 325°F. oven for 30 to 35 minutes, or until just barely set. Remove from oven and place pan on a wire rack. While still warm, cut into squares. Dust with powdered sugar, if desired. Makes 4 dozen.

Chocolate Delice

These souffle-like brownies are sinfully rich and a pushover for seconds.

10 ozs. semi-sweet chocolate
6 eggs, separated, at room temperature
1 tsp. vanilla
1/4 cup sugar

2 tbs. all-purpose flour
1/4 tsp. salt
1/2 cup butter, at room temperature

Melt chocolate in double boiler over hot water. Let cool slightly. Beat egg yolks until light and pale yellow in color. Beat in vanilla, 1 tablespoon of the sugar, flour, salt and butter. Stir in chocolate and mix until smooth. Beat egg whites until soft peaks form. Add remaining 3 tablespoons sugar. Continue beating until stiff. Fold beaten egg whites into chocolate mixture. Turn into a buttered 9 x 13-inch baking pan. Bake in a 375°F. oven for 15 minutes, or until the center is barely set. Let cool, then chill. Cut Into squares. Let warm to room temperature before serving. Makes 3 dozen.

Applesauce Brownies

The fruity moistness of applesauce makes these chocolate bars a good traveler. The mixing is swift—everything goes together right in a saucepan.

2/3 cup butter
2 ozs. unsweetened chocolate
1 cup sugar
1 tsp. vanilla
2 eggs
3/4 cup all-purpose flour

1/4 cup wheat germ
1/2 tsp. EACH baking powder and salt
1/4 cup applesauce
1/2 cup chopped walnuts, pecans, or almonds
powdered sugar for topping

Melt butter and chocolate over low heat using a heavy saucepan or a double boiler over hot water. Remove from heat and stir in sugar and vanilla. Add eggs, one at a time, beating well after each addition. In a bowl, stir together flour, wheat germ, baking powder and salt. Add to butter mixture alternately with applesauce. Stir in nuts. Turn into greased 9 x 13-inch baking pan. Bake at 350°F. for 20 minutes, or until set and golden brown. Let cool. Cut into squares and dust with powdered sugar. Omit powdered sugar if cookies are to be stored or shipped. Makes about 35 cookies.

Chocolate Chip Butterscotch Bars

This timeless cookie is enriched with whole wheat flour and wheat germ. Serve in large squares with a dollop of vanilla ice cream for a rich dessert.

3/4 cup butter, at room temperature
2 cups firmly packed brown sugar
1 tsp. vanilla
2 eggs
1 cup all-purpose flour
1 cup whole wheat flour

1 tsp. baking powder
1/2 tsp. baking soda
1/4 tsp. salt
1/2 cup chopped walnuts
1 pkg. (6 ozs.) semi-sweet chocolate chips
1/3 cup wheat germ

Beat butter and sugar together until creamy. Mix in vanilla and eggs. Stir together flours, baking powder, soda, and salt. Add to creamed mixture. Beat well. By hand, stir in nuts, chocolate chips and wheat germ, mixing well. Spread into a greased 9 x 13-inch pan. Bake in a 350ºF. oven for 20 to 25 minutes, or until set and golden brown. Let cool on a rack, then cut into squares. Makes about 40 cookies.

Chocolate Rum Strips

These chewy cocoa bars are laced with rum and almonds. For variety substitute the popular after dinner liqueur "Amaretto" for the rum.

1 cup whole blanched almonds or filberts
2 eggs, at room temperature
3/4 cup sugar
1/3 cup unsweetened cocoa

1/2 cup cake flour
1/4 tsp. salt
2 tbs. dark rum OR Amaretto
powdered sugar

Using a food processor or blender, grind almonds finely, making about 1-1/4 cups ground nuts. Using an electric mixer or wire whisk beat eggs until light and lemon-colored. Add sugar. Continue beating until thick. Add nuts, cocoa, flour, salt and rum. Mix well. Spread into a well buttered 7 x 11-inch baking pan. Bake in a 350°F. oven for 20 to 25 minutes, or until a toothpick inserted into center comes out clean. Let cool slightly, then dust with powdered sugar shaken through a sieve. Cut into strips or squares. Makes about 3 dozen.

Chocolate Peanut Bars

1 cup butter, at room temperature
1/2 cup granulated sugar
1-1/2 cups firmly packed brown sugar
2 eggs, separated at room temperature
1 tsp. vanilla
2 cups all-purpose flour

1 tsp. baking powder
1/4 tsp. baking soda
1/4 tsp. salt
1 pkg. (6 ozs.) semi-sweet chocolate chips
1 cup Spanish peanuts

64

Beat butter, granulated sugar and 1/2 cup of the brown sugar together until creamy. Beat in egg yolks and vanilla. In a separate bowl, stir together flour, baking powder, soda and salt. Add to creamed mixture. Beat well. Pat out dough into a greased 10 x 15-inch baking pan. Sprinkle with chocolate chips, pressing in gently. Beat egg whites until soft peaks form. Beat in remaining 1 cup brown sugar. Continue beating until stiff. Spread meringue mixture over top of chocolate chips. Sprinkle with peanuts. Bake in a 350°F. oven for 20 to 25 minutes, or until set and golden brown. Let cool, then cut into bars. Makes about 5 dozen.

Hints: If using food processor, DON'T make meringue in it. Use electric beaters or wire whisk.

Chocolate Chip Dream Bars

Crust:
   1-1/2 cups all-purpose flour
   3/4 cup firmly packed
      light brown sugar
   1/2 cup butter or margarine,
      at room temperature

Topping:
   3 eggs
   1-1/2 cups firmly packed light brown sugar
   1 tsp. vanilla
   1/4 tsp. salt
   3 tbs. all-purpose flour
   1/2 tsp. baking powder
   1 pkg. (6 ozs.) semi-sweet chocolate chips
   3/4 cup finely chopped walnuts, pecans, or almonds

For crust, mix together flour, sugar, and butter until crumbly. Pat into a buttered 10 x 15-inch baking pan, pressing down firmly. Bake in a 375°F. oven for 12 minutes, or until lightly browned. Meanwhile prepare topping. Beat eggs with an electric mixer or wire whip until light. Beat in sugar, vanilla, salt, flour and baking powder. By hand, fold in chocolate chips and nuts. Spread batter over baked crust and return to oven. Bake 10 minutes longer, or just until puffed and golden brown. Let cool and cut into bars. Makes 5 dozen.

Hint: For plain, old-fashioned Dream Bars, omit the chocolate chips.

Chocolate Cheese Sticks

1 large pkg. (8 ozs.)
   cream cheese, at room temperature
3/4 cup butter, at room temperature
3/4 cup sugar
1 tsp. vanilla
2 cups all-purpose flour

1/2 tsp. baking powder
1 tsp. grated orange peel
1 pkg. (6 ozs.) semi-sweet
   chocolate chips
1/2 cup chopped toasted almonds,
   filberts or walnuts (optional)

66   Beat cream cheese and butter together until light and creamy. Add sugar and vanilla. Beat well. In a separate bowl, stir together flour and baking powder. Add to creamed mixture. Beat well. Add orange peel, mixing until blended. Spread into an ungreased 10 x 15-inch baking pan. Bake in a 375°F. oven for 15 minutes, or until set and lightly browned on the edges. Remove from oven and sprinkle with chocolate chips. Let stand a few minutes to melt. Then spread with a spatula to coat evenly. Sprinkle with nuts. Cool, then cut into bars. Cut into 1-1/2 inch lengthwise strips, then into 2-inch bars. Makes about 4 dozen.

Cheesecake Confections

Orange zest and chocolate enhance these cheesecake bars centered between a walnut base and topping.

2/3 cup firmly packed brown sugar
1 cup chopped walnuts
2 cups all-purpose flour
2/3 cup butter, melted
2 pkgs. (8 ozs. each) softened cream cheese
1/2 cup granulated sugar

2 eggs
2 tbs. orange juice concentrate,
   thawed and undiluted
2 tbs. milk
1 pkg. (6 ozs.) semi-sweet
   chocolate chips

Mix together brown sugar, nuts, and flour. Add melted butter and mix until light and crumbly. Reserve 2 cups for topping and press remainder into a greased 9 x 13-inch baking pan. Bake in a 350°F. oven for 12 minutes, or until lightly browned. Beat together cream cheese and sugar until smooth. Add eggs, orange juice concentrate and milk. Beat well. By hand, stir in chocolate chips. Pour cheese mixture onto baked crust. Top with reserved crumbs. Bake for 25 to 30 minutes or just until set. Let cool. Then cut into squares. Makes 5 dozen.

Butterscotch Bars

For a really quick treat, try these bars. They go together in a jiffy.

1/2 cup butter
2 cups firmly packed brown sugar
2 eggs
1 tsp. vanilla
1 cup all-purpose flour
2 tsp. baking powder
1/2 tsp. salt
1 cup slivered almonds

68

In a large saucepan, melt butter over medium heat. Stir in brown sugar until absorbed. Remove mixture from heat. Let cool slightly. Add eggs, one at a time, mixing well after each addition. Stir in vanilla. In a bowl, stir together flour, baking powder and salt. Add to mixture in saucepan. Add half of the nuts. Stir well. Turn mixture into a greased 9 x 13-inch baking pan. Sprinkle with remaining nuts. Bake in a 350°F. oven for 20 to 25 minutes, or until golden brown. Makes 4 dozen.

Almond Crunch Bars

These golden nut bars are ideal with fresh strawberries or a juicy peach or pear.

1/2 cup butter, at room temperature
2/3 cup sugar
1 egg, separated
1/2 tsp. vanilla

1/4 tsp. almond extract
1 cup all-purpose flour
1/2 tsp. ground cinnamon
1/3 cup sliced almonds

Beat butter and 1/2 cup of sugar together until creamy. Beat in egg yolk, vanilla and almond extract. Add flour, mixing until smooth. Pat into a buttered 9-inch square baking pan. Beat egg white with electric mixer or wire whisk until soft peaks form. Beat in remaining sugar and cinnamon. Continue beating until stiff and glossy. Spread over dough and sprinkle with almonds. Bake in a 375°F. oven for 20 minutes, or until lightly browned. Cut into squares. Makes 3 dozen.

Coconut Honey Bars

This healthful, cake-like bar retains a moist chewiness for several days. In fact, its flavor improves after two or three days.

1/2 cup butter, at room temperature
3/4 cup firmly packed brown sugar
6 tbs. honey
2 eggs
3/4 cup whole wheat flour
1 tsp. baking powder

1/2 tsp. salt
1 cup flaked coconut
1/2 cup chopped almonds,
    walnuts or pecans
1 cup bran flakes or rolled oats

Beat butter and sugar together until creamy. Mix in honey and eggs, beating until smooth. In a separate bowl, stir together flour, baking powder and salt. Add to creamed mixture. Stir well. By hand, stir in coconut, nuts and bran flakes. Mix well. Spread batter into a greased 7 x 11-inch baking pan. Bake in a 350°F. oven for 30 minutes, or until set and golden brown. Let cool. Cut into squares. Makes 28 cookies.

Butterscotch Toppers

1/2 cup butter, at room temperature
3/4 cup firmly packed brown sugar
dash salt
1-3/4 cups all-purpose flour

Topping:
  1 pkg. (6 ozs.)
    butterscotch bits
  1/4 cup light corn syrup
  2 tbs. butter
  2 cups finely chopped
    walnuts or pecans

Mix together butter, brown sugar, salt and flour until crumbly. Pat into the bottom of a greased and floured 9 x 13-inch baking pan. Bake in a 375°F. oven for 10 minutes. Meanwhile, combine butterscotch bits, corn syrup, 2 tablespoons butter, and 1 tablespoon water in the top of a double boiler. Place over hot water and stir until butterscotch bits and butter are melted and mixture is smooth. Mix in nuts. Spread over baked cookie base and return to 350°F. oven for 10 minutes longer. Let cool slightly. Cut into squares while still warm. Makes 4 dozen.

German Honey Bars

A baked on honey-almond topping glazes these Continental cookie bars. A nice cookie to serve with fresh fruit for dessert.

1-3/4 cups all-purpose flour
1/2 cup sugar
2 tsp. baking powder
1/2 cup butter, at room temperature

Honey Topping:
1/3 cup sugar
1/4 cup honey
1/4 cup whipping cream
1/4 cup all-purpose flour
1 cup sliced almonds

Place flour, 1/2 cup sugar, baking powder and butter in a mixing bowl. Mix until crumbly. Pat into a buttered 10 x 15-inch baking pan. Bake in a 350°F. oven for 10 minutes. Meanwhile, make Honey Topping. Place 1/3 cup sugar, honey and cream together in a saucepan. Bring to a boil and cook until the temperature reaches 190°F. on a candy thermometer. Remove from heat and whisk in flour. Stir in nuts. Spread over crust and continue baking 10 minutes longer, or until golden brown. Let cool on wire rack, then cut into bars. Makes about 4-1/2 dozen.

Banana Chocolate Chip Bars

1/2 cup butter, at room temperature
3/4 cup firmly packed brown sugar
1 cup mashed bananas
   (about 2 medium-size)
1/2 tsp. vanilla
1-1/4 cups. all-purpose flour
1/2 cup wheat germ
1/2 tsp. baking soda

1/4 tsp. salt
1 pkg. (6 ozs.) semi-sweet
   chocolate chips
3/4 cup chopped
   walnuts or pecans
2 tbs. granulated sugar
1-1/2 tsp. cinnamon

Beat butter and brown sugar together until creamy. Beat in bananas and vanilla. In separate bowl, stir together flour, wheat germ, soda and salt. Add to creamed mixture, beating well. By hand, stir in chocolate chips and half of the nuts. Spread mixture in a greased 9 x 13-inch baking pan. Sprinkle with remaining nuts. Mix together sugar and cinnamon and sprinkle over nuts. Bake in a 350°F. oven for 18 to 20 minutes, or until toothpick inserted into center comes out clean. Makes about 3 dozen bars.

Mincemeat Bars

This versatile bar cookie is excellent filled with dates, as well.

3/4 cup butter, at room temperature
1 cup firmly packed brown sugar
1-3/4 cups all-purpose flour
3/4 tsp. salt
1/2 tsp. baking soda

1-1/2 cups rolled oats
1 jar (28 ozs.) prepared mincemeat
2 tsp. grated orange peel
1/2 cup chopped walnuts or pecans

Beat butter and sugar together until creamy. In separate bowl, stir together flour, salt and soda. Add to creamed mixture. Beat well. Stir in oats. Press half of the mixture into a greased 9 x13-inch baking pan. Mix together the mincemeat, orange peel and nuts and spread over bottom layer. Crumble remaining oatmeal mixture, over top pressing lightly. Bake in a 400ºF. oven for 25 minutes, or until golden brown. Let cool, then cut into squares. Makes about 3-1/2 dozen.

Hints: for date variation, place 3 cups chopped dates, 1/2 cup sugar and 1-1/2 cups water in a saucepan. Cook over medium-low heat, stirring occasionally, for about 10 minutes. Substitute for mincemeat in filling. Add orange peel and nuts, if desired.

Orange Glazed Mincemeat Bars

This frosted holiday cookie makes a nourishing treat.

3/4 cup butter, at room temperature
3/4 cup firmly packed brown sugar
2 eggs
1 tsp. vanilla
1 cup all-purpose flour
2/3 cup whole wheat flour
2/3 cup wheat germ
1 tsp. cinnamon
3/4 tsp. soda
1/2 tsp. salt
1/2 cup chopped pecans or walnuts
1 pkg. (9 ozs.) condensed mincemeat, crumbled
Orange Glaze, see next page

Beat butter and sugar together until creamy. Beat in eggs and vanilla. In separate bowl, stir together flours, wheat germ, cinnamon, soda and salt. Add to creamed mixture. By hand, stir in nuts and mincemeat. Spread into a greased 10 x15-inch baking pan. Bake in a 375°F. oven for 15 to 18 minutes, or until set and golden brown. Let cool on wire rack 2 minutes. Frost with Orange Glaze. Let cool completely. Cut into bars or squares. Makes about 3 dozen.

Orange Glaze

1-1/2 cups powdered sugar
2 tbs. orange juice concentrate, thawed
1 tsp. grated orange peel

Combine all ingredients and mix together until smooth.

Date Nut Strips

The ground nuts actually serve as flour, along with cracker crumbs, in these chewy bars.

3 eggs, at room temperature
3/4 cup firmly packed light brown sugar
1/2 tsp. vanilla
1/2 cup crushed graham cracker crumbs
1/2 tsp. baking powder

dash salt
3/4 cup finely ground
   walnuts or pecans
3/4 cup dates, cut finely
powdered sugar

78

Beat eggs until thick and lemon colored. Beat in sugar and vanilla. In a separate bowl, stir together cracker crumbs, baking powder and salt. Add to egg mixture. Stir in nuts and dates. Turn into a greased 9-inch square baking pan. Bake in a 350°F. oven for 20 to 25 minutes, or until set. Let cool, then cut into strips and roll in powdered sugar. Makes about 2 dozen.

Hints: If using food processor, grind nuts with 2 table-spoons brown sugar (deducted from 3/4 cup) to keep them fluffy. **DON'T** beat eggs in processor. Use electric beaters or a wire whisk.

Date Meringue Bars

1/2 cup butter, at room temperature
3 cups firmly packed light brown sugar
3 eggs, separated
1 cup all-purpose flour
1 tsp. baking powder

1/2 tsp. salt
2 cups quick-cooking rolled oats
2 cups pitted dates, chopped
1 cup water
2 tsp. grated orange peel

Beat butter and 1-1/2 cups sugar together until light and creamy. Mix in egg yolks, one at a time, beating well after each addition. In a separate bowl, stir together flour, baking powder and 1/4 teaspoon of the salt. Add to creamed mixture. Beat well. Stir in oats. Pat into the bottom of a greased 9 x 13-inch baking pan. Place dates, water and orange peel in a saucepan. Bring to a boil, and simmer 5 minutes. Cool slightly, then spread over crust mixture. Beat egg whites until foamy. Add remaining 1/4 teaspoon salt and beat until soft peaks form. Add remaining 1-1/2 cups brown sugar gradually and beat until thick and glossy. Spread over date layer. Bake in a 350°F. oven for 25 to 30 minutes, or until meringue is set. Let cool and cut into bars. Makes about 4 dozen.

Hints: If using food processor, prepare crust ONLY in processor.

Apricot Bars

2/3 cup dried apricots
1/2 cup butter or margarine,
   at room temperature
1/4 cup granulated sugar
1 cup all-purpose flour
2 eggs
1 cup firmly packed brown sugar

1/2 tsp. vanilla
1/3 cup all-purpose flour
1 tsp. baking powder
1/4 tsp. salt
1/2 cup chopped walnuts or pecans
powdered sugar (optional)

80

Rinse apricots and cover with water in small saucepan. Simmer, covered, for 10 minutes. Drain, cool and chop. Beat butter, granulated sugar and 1 cup flour together until crumbly. Pat into a greased 8-inch square baking pan. Bake in a 350°F. oven for 15 minutes, or until lightly browned. Beat eggs until light. Beat in brown sugar and vanilla. In a separate bowl, stir together 1/3 cup flour, baking powder and salt. Add to egg mixture. Beat well. Add nuts and apricots. Spread on the baked layer and continue baking 25 to 30 minutes, or until set. Let cool in pan. Cut into bars or squares. If desired, dust with powdered sugar. Makes about 2-1/2 dozen.

Hints: If using food processor, let whole apricots and whole nuts chop into batter as they blend.

Lemon Bars

These citrus bars have a tart-sweet flavor much like old-fashioned lemon curd.

Crust:
   2 cups all-purpose flour
   1/2 cup powdered sugar
   1 cup butter, chilled
Topping:
   4 eggs
   1-1/2 cups sugar

1/4 cup flour
6 tbs. lemon juice
2 tbs. grated lemon peel
1 tsp. baking powder
1/2 tsp. salt
powdered sugar

For Crust, mix together flour, sugar, and butter until crumbly. Pat into bottom and 1/4-inch up the sides of a buttered 9 x 13-inch baking pan. Bake in a 350°F. oven for 15 to 20 minutes, or until lightly browned. Meanwhile, prepare Topping. Beat eggs slightly. In a separate bowl, stir together sugar and flour. Add to eggs. Beat well. Add lemon juice, peel, baking powder, and salt. Beat until smooth. Pour over baked crust. Return to oven and bake 25 to 30 minutes longer, or until just set. Sprinkle with powdered sugar while hot. Let cool and cut in bars. Makes 4 dozen.

Linzer Bars

The flavor duo of almonds and raspberries is seductive in this Austrian specialty. For variety, try substituting apricot jam for the raspberry. Serve in large squares for a great dessert.

1 cup butter, at room temperature
1 cup sugar
2 eggs
1 tsp. grated lemon peel
2 cups all-purpose flour
1 cup almonds, ground

1/2 tsp. cinnamon
1 tbs. unsweetened cocoa
1/4 tsp. salt
1-1/2 cups raspberry jam
Streusel Topping, see next page

Beat butter and sugar together until creamy. Add eggs and lemon peel, beating until smooth. In a separate bowl, stir together flour, almonds, cinnamon, cocoa, and salt. Add dry ingredients to creamed mixture. Mix thoroughly. Spread into an ungreased 10 x 15-inch baking pan, making a 1/4-inch edge on the sides. Freeze pan 10 minutes to firm up crust. Spread surface with jam and crumble Streusel Topping over top. Bake in a 325°F. oven for 40 minutes, or until golden brown. Let cool on rack and cut into squares. Makes about 5 dozen.

Streusel Topping

3 tbs. sugar
1/3 cup margarine, at room temperature
2/3 cup flour
1 tsp. unsweetened cocoa

Place all ingredients in a mixing bowl. With your fingers, an electric mixer or a food processor, mix until crumbly.

Hints: If using a food processor, grind nuts with 2 table- spoons flour (deducted from 2 cups) first. Remove from bowl. Prepare Streusel Topping in processor. Remove from bowl and set aside. Prepare dough.

Refrigerator Cookies

These cookies are among the easiest to bake. Once the dough has been made, simply shape it into rolls and refrigerate it until it has become firm enough to slice. For variety, pack the dough into juice cans, whose ends have been removed. This will produce uniformly shaped cookies.

It is nice to have rolls of dough in the refrigerator handy for unexpected guests or the children's after school snack. Well-wrapped rolls keep for up to 2 weeks. The dough may also be frozen for up to 3 months. If you prefer extra thin and crispy cookies, freeze the dough until it is quite firm before you bake it. Freezing allows you to slice the rolls wafer thin. To achieve the best results, use a sharp slicing knife.

Lemon Nut Wafers

The oil in the lemon is drawn out and thus the flavor of these cookies intensified by first mashing the peel with sugar.

1 tbs. grated lemon peel
1 cup sugar
1/2 cup butter, at room temperature
1 tbs. lemon juice
2 cups all-purpose flour

1/8 tsp. salt
1 tsp. baking powder
1 cup finely chopped toasted
   walnuts or pecans

Place lemon peel in a small bowl. Add 1 teaspoon of the sugar and mash with the back of a spoon. Beat butter and remaining sugar together until creamy. Add lemon juice and lemon peel. In a separate bowl, stir together flour, salt and baking powder. Add to creamed mixture. Beat well. Stir in nuts. Shape into two rolls, each about 2 inches in diameter. Wrap in foil, waxed paper or plastic wrap and chill until firm. Slice very thinly and place on an ungreased baking sheet. Bake in a 375°F. oven for 8 to 10 minutes, or until golden brown. Makes about 4 to 5 dozen.

Caramel Slices

This cookie is a childhood favorite. Mother often filled the cookie "can" with these crispy slices.

1 cup butter, at room temperature
2 cups firmly packed brown sugar
2 eggs
1 tsp. vanilla
1 tsp. EACH baking soda and cream of tartar
3-1/4 cups all-purpose flour
1 cup chopped walnuts or pecans

Beat butter and sugar together until light and creamy. Mix in eggs and vanilla. In a separate bowl, stir together baking soda, cream of tartar and flour. Add to creamed mixture, mixing until blended. Stir in nuts. Shape into rolls, 2-1/2 inches in diameter. Wrap in foil, waxed paper or plastic wrap and chill until firm. Cut into 3/8-inch thick slices and place on a greased baking sheet. Bake in a 350°F. oven for 8 to 10 minutes, or until golden brown. Makes about 5 dozen cookies.

Hawaiian Shortbread

Powdered sugar covers these crispy wafers, while macadamia nuts lend their sublime crunch.

1 cup butter, at room temperature
1/3 cup sugar
1 tsp. vanilla
2 cups all-purpose flour
1/4 tsp. salt

1/2 cup very finely chopped
  macadamia nuts or almonds
2 cups flaked coconut
3/4 cup powdered sugar

88

Beat butter and sugar together until creamy. Mix in vanilla. Gradually add flour and salt, beating until smooth. Mix in nuts and coconut. Beat until well distributed. Divide dough in half. Shape into two 1-1/2-inch thick rolls. Wrap in waxed paper, foil, or plastic wrap. Chill 1 hour. Cut into 1/4-inch thick slices. Place on a greased baking sheet. Bake in a 325°F. oven for 12 minutes, or until lightly browned. Slip a sheet of waxed paper beneath cooling racks. Transfer cookies to racks and let cool three to four minutes. Then dust tops of cookies with powdered sugar, shaken through a sieve. Let cool completely. Store in an airtight container. Makes 4 dozen.

Hint: Process nuts before creaming butter and sugar, OR add them to batter and let them chop as they blend into batter.

Collect a treasury of your favorite cooking subjects with the new "Kitchen Companion."

INTRODUCTORY OFFER — ONLY $6.95

(See other side)

A Real Time Saver

Holds cookbook open so you can easily keep your place while cooking

Protects your cookbooks and brings them together in one handy location

Durable modern clear plastic design

Holds up to ten Nitty Gritty Cookbooks

Compact
- fits almost anywhere in your kitchen
- can be placed on counter or mounted under kitchen shelf (instructions and screws included)
- saves space— only 5-7/8" x 6-1/2" x 7-3/4"
- can be stacked one on top of another in a bookshelf to get twice the books in the same space

SPECIAL INTRODUCTORY OFFER — ONLY $6.95 (Retail value $15.95 — You save $9.00!)

Now, you can always have an easy delicious recipe within reach for any occasion. This new Kitchen Companion allows you to assemble up to ten of your favorite cooking subjects in one place for easy reference. Even if you have a cabinet full of cookbooks, a new Kitchen Companion filled with popular Nitty Gritty Cookbooks will save you time and guarantee you easy meals you can be proud of! Money-back 30 Day Guarantee. (Books and other items shown are not included in this offer.)

nitty gritty® cookbooks

P.O. Box 910-Dept. CCA-6
Lomita, CA 90717

Chocolate Almond Circles

This German refrigerator cookie has a charming speckled appearance.

1 cup whole almonds
3 ozs. semi-sweet chocolate
1 cup all-purpose flour
1/2 cup butter, at room temperature

1/3 cup sugar
1 tsp. vanilla
1 egg

Whirl almonds in blender or food processor or grate in a nut grater until they are the consistency of cornmeal. Turn into a mixing bowl. Place chocolate in blender or food processor. Whirl until finely grated. Add to bowl with almonds. Add flour, butter, sugar, vanilla and egg to nuts and chocolate. Mix until dough is just blended. Turn out on a lightly floured board and roll out into a cylinder about 2 1/4 inches in diameter. Wrap in waxed paper, foil or plastic wrap and chill until firm. Slice as thinly as possible and place on a greased baking sheet. Bake in a 350°F. oven for 10 to 12 minutes, or until set. Remove to wire racks and let cool. Makes 3 dozen.

89

Three Grain Almond Wafers

A trio of grains enrich these healthful cookies.

1 cup rolled oats
2/3 cup butter, at room temperature
1-1/4 cups firmly packed brown sugar
1 egg
1 tbs. instant coffee powder
1 tsp. vanilla
1 cup whole wheat flour
1 tsp. baking powder
1/3 cup rye flour
1/3 cup chopped almonds

Spread oats evenly on a cookie sheet. Place under broiler for 3 to 5 minutes, stirring frequently. Broil until lightly toasted. Remove from oven and let cool. Set aside. Beat butter and sugar together until creamy. Add egg, coffee powder and vanilla. Beat well. In a separate bowl, stir together oats, flour, baking powder and rye flour. Add to creamed mixture. Beat well. Stir in nuts. Shape into 2 rolls, each about 1-3/4 inches in diameter. Wrap in foil, waxed paper or plastic wrap. Chill until firm. Slice roll into 1/8-inch thick rounds. Place on a lightly greased baking sheet. Bake in a 350°F. oven for about 8 minutes, or until golden brown. Immediately remove to wire racks and let cool. Makes about 3-1/2 dozen.

Spiced Filbert Wafers

This cinnamon-spiced refrigerator cookie is perfect with a fresh fruit compote.

1 cup butter, at room temperature
1 cup firmly packed brown sugar
2 cups all-purpose flour
2 tsp. cinnamon
1/4 tsp. baking soda
1/4 cup sour cream
3/4 cup finely chopped lightly toasted filberts

92

Beat butter and sugar together until creamy. In a separate bowl, stir together flour and cinnamon. In a small bowl, blend soda into the sour cream. Add dry ingredients to creamed mixture alternately with sour cream. Beat well. Mix in toasted nuts. Shape into rolls, about 2-1/2 inches in diameter. Wrap in waxed paper, plastic wrap or foil and chill until firm. Slice 1/8-inch thick and place on ungreased baking sheets. Bake in a 350°F. oven for 8 to 10 minutes, or until golden brown. Makes about 6 dozen.

Vanilla Butter Wafers

These French butter wafers have a unique fragile texture. A split vanilla bean lends a wonderful aromatic flavor. If unavailable, substitute 1 teaspoon vanilla extract.

2-inch piece vanilla bean, split
1-1/4 cups unsifted powdered sugar
1 cup butter, at room temperature
1 egg

2 cups all-purpose flour
1 tsp. EACH baking soda
   and cream of tartar

Bury the split vanilla bean in the sugar in a covered container for 1 day, or longer. Remove bean just before using sugar. Beat butter until creamy. Beat in vanilla-flavored sugar, until light and fluffy. Add egg. In separate bowl, sift together flour, soda and cream of tartar. Add to creamed mixture. Mix well. Shape into a 2-inch round roll. Wrap in plastic wrap, waxed paper or foil and chill 1 hour or longer. Slice into 1/4-inch thick rounds. Place on ungreased baking sheets. Bake in a 350°F. oven for 8 to 10 minutes, or until golden brown on the edges. Makes about 3 dozen.

Pinwheels

In these cookies, two different colored doughs are rolled together like a jelly roll. They appear difficult to make, but are not.

1 ounce unsweetened chocolate
1/2 cup butter
3/4 cup sugar
1/2 tsp. vanilla
1 egg
1-3/4 cups all-purpose flour
1/2 tsp. baking powder
1/4 tsp. salt
1 tsp. instant coffee powder
1/4 tsp. almond extract

In the top of a double boiler, melt chocolate over hot water. Set aside to cool. Beat butter and sugar together until creamy. Mix in vanilla and egg. In a separate bowl, stir together flour, baking powder and salt. Add to creamed mixture. Beat well. Divide dough between 2 bowls. Add melted chocolate and coffee powder to one bowl. To other bowl add almond extract. Tear off 4 pieces of waxed paper, each about 17 inches long. Place one ball of dough on a piece of paper. Top with another piece of paper. Roll to a 14 x 9-inch rectangle. Repeat with remaining ball of dough. Remove top piece of paper from both rectangles of dough. Invert chocolate dough over white dough, carefully aligning them. Once chocolate dough comes into contact with white dough, it will adhere. Remove top sheet of paper from chocolate layer. Using bottom sheet of paper (under white dough) roll dough as for a jelly roll. This will create the pinwheel affect. Wrap roll in waxed paper and refrigerate until very firm, 1 to 2 hours. Slice roll into 1/4-inch rounds. Place 1 inch apart on an ungreased baking sheet. Bake at 350°F. for about 12 minutes. Makes 4 to 5 dozen.

Rolled and Cut-out Cookies

What child doesn't love to adorn cookie cut-outs with colored sugar sprinkles and dragees, or press raisin buttons and eyes on gingerbread boys? These are joyous tasks for youngsters, especially pleasing when a collection of their creations is carried off to classmates for a school party.

A common problem when working with rolled and cut-out dough is using too much flour. Here are several ways to avoid this: (1) Use a pastry cloth and a stockinette covered rolling pin; (2) For especially sticky dough, roll between two pieces of waxed paper or plastic wrap; (3) Use cookie cutters that interlock, thus making the maximum cuts from each sheet of dough; (4) Roll dough directly on baking sheet. Make cut-outs and lift surplus scraps of dough off. Excess flour will cause your cookies to become tough and less buttery, so adopt any method which helps you prevent using too much flour.

If your cookie cutter has a tendency to stick to the dough, dip it in either powdered sugar or warm water before you cut each cookie.

Lemon Diamonds

Diamonds are a festive way to cut this Austrian almond cookie. Use a fluted cutter or wheel for an attractive edge.

1 egg white
1 cup sugar
1-1/2 cup finely ground blanched almonds
1-1/2 tsp. grated lemon peel
2 tbs. lemon juice

Glaze:
1/2 cup powdered sugar
2 tsp. lemon juice

Beat egg white slightly with fork or wire whisk. Mix in sugar, almonds, lemon peel and juice. Pat out mixture to 1/4 inch thickness on a baking sheet sprinkled with granulated·sugar. Sprinkle dough with additional sugar. Using a pastry wheel, cut it into 2 x 1-inch diamond shapes. Let dry for 8 hours, or overnight. Place on a greased baking sheet. Bake in a 350°F. oven for 15 minutes, or until lightly colored. Transfer to a rack and let cool. For glaze, combine powdered sugar and lemon juice and brush on top of cookies. Makes 2-1/2 dozen.

Sugar Cookies

This is a holiday favorite to cut into stars, bells, trees and angels. Adorn them with colored sugar sprinkles or tinted frosting.

1/2 cup EACH butter and margarine
  (or all butter), at room temperature
1-1/4 cups sugar
2 eggs
1 tsp. vanilla

1/4 tsp. almond extract
3-1/2 cups all-purpose flour
1 tsp. baking powder
1/4 tsp. salt

99

Beat butter until creamy. Beat in sugar, eggs, vanilla and almond extract. In a separate bowl, stir together flour, baking powder and salt. Add to creamed mixture. Beat well. Cover and chill at least 1 hour. Roll out dough to 1/8 inch thickness on a lightly floured board. Cut into desired shapes. Place on greased baking sheets. Sprinkle with colored sugar if desired. Bake in a 400°F. oven for 6 to 8 minutes, or until lightly browned. Remove immediately to wire racks and let cool. Makes about 4 dozen cookies.

Hint: These cookies also make charming placecards for a children's party. Cut out into rounds or hearts and frost each one with the name of the guest.

Fauchon's Hearts

Edmond Bory, the dashing owner of the elite Parisian gourmet shop named Fauchon, shares this favorite from his shop.

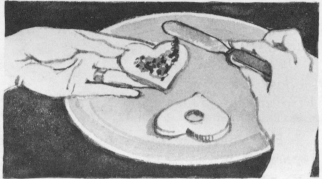

3/4 cup butter, at room temperature
1/2 cup powdered sugar
1/2 tsp. vanilla
1 egg
3/4 cup finely ground blanched almonds
2 cups all-purpose flour
raspberry or gooseberry jam or jelly
powdered sugar

100

Beat butter and powdered sugar together until creamy. Beat in vanilla and egg. Add almonds and flour, mixing to incorporate. Wrap in waxed paper and chill 1 hour. Roll out on a lightly floured board and cut into heart-shaped cookies. Use a small (1/2-inch) circle to cut out the center of half of the cookies. Place on a lightly greased bak-

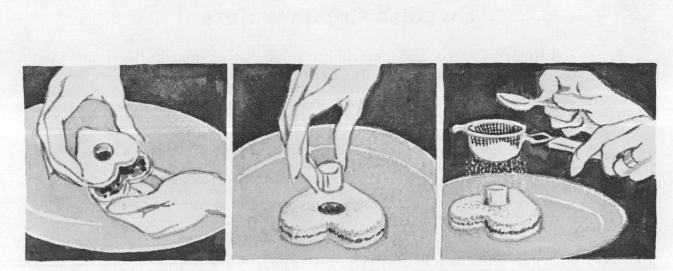

ing sheet. Bake in a 375°F. oven for 6 to 8 minutes, or until cookies are just beginning to turn golden brown. Transfer to a rack and let cool. Sandwich cookies together with warmed jam or jelly. Use one whole heart and one centerless heart per sandwich. Cover hole with object that was used to cut it. Dust tops of cookies with sifted powdered sugar then uncover center. Makes 3 dozen cookies.

Swedish Cream Wafers

Sandwich together these puff paste-like rounds with tinted buttercream filling. They make perfect party fare for a bridal shower or other festive occasions.

1 cup butter, chilled and cut
   into 1/2-inch cubes
2 cups all-purpose flour
1/2 cup whipping cream
granulated sugar

Buttercream Filling:
1/4 cup butter, at room temperature
1 cup powdered sugar
1 egg yolk
1 tsp. vanilla OR 1/2 tsp. almond extract
drops of food coloring, if desired

Beat butter and flour together until a crumb-like mixture forms. Add cream and mix until mixture clings together. Shape into a ball. Wrap in plastic wrap or waxed paper and chill 1 hour. Roll out 1/3 of the dough at a time on a floured board to about 1/8-inch thick. Cut into rounds about 1-1/2 inches in diameter. Prick with a fork, as you would a pie crust. Transfer to waxed paper which has been heavily coated with granulated sugar. Turn cookie rounds to coat evenly with sugar. Place on ungreased baking sheet about 1 inch apart. Bake in a 375°F. oven for 8 minutes, or until golden brown. Transfer to wire racks and let cool. Prepare filling. Combine all ingredients in a small mixing bowl, or processor and beat until smooth. Just before serving the cookies, fill them with buttercream. Makes about 2 dozen.

Hint: If using a food processor for cookie dough, be careful not to overprocess. It takes just a few seconds to mix.

Cinnamon Hearts

Mrs. Herbert Hoover's Chinese cook became famous for these spicy, nut-topped cookies.

1/2 cup butter, at room temperature
1 cup sugar
1 egg
1 tsp. vanilla

1-1/2 cups all-purpose flour
1 tsp. EACH baking powder and cinnamon
1/2 cup sugar
1/2 cup chopped walnuts

104

Cream butter and 1 cup sugar together. Add egg and vanilla. Mix well. In a separate bowl, stir together flour and baking powder. Add to creamed mixture. Beat thoroughly. Roll dough out to 3/16-inch thick, on a floured board. Cut out heart shapes or scalloped edged rounds. Place on greased baking sheet. Combine cinnamon with 1/2 cup sugar. Mix well. Sprinkle cinnamon-sugar over cookies. Sprinkle with nuts. Bake in a 350°F. oven for 8 to 10 minutes, or until golden brown. Remove to wire racks to cool. Makes about 2-1/2 dozen.

Brown Sugar Shortbreads

Use a cookie cutter to cut out these golden brown shortbreads. They keep especially well.

1 cup butter, at room temperature
3/4 cup firmly packed brown sugar
2-1/4 cups cake flour
powdered sugar for dusting

Beat butter and brown sugar together until creamy. Add flour, mixing until it forms a solid ball. Roll out on a lightly floured board to 1/4-inch thickness. Cut out with fancy cutters or with a pastry wheel. Place on ungreased baking sheets. Bake in a 325°F. oven for 15 to 18 minutes, or until set. Makes about 3 dozen.

Hint: If using food processor, be careful not to overprocess dough.

Lemon Oat Crisps

These lemon wafers may either be sliced and baked, or rolled and cut out into stars, hearts, or scalloped rounds. Coarse sugar lends a crackly and delicious finish on top.

1/2 cup butter, at room temperature
1 cup sugar
1 egg
1/2 tsp. EACH lemon extract and vanilla
2 tsp. grated lemon peel
1/4 cup sour cream
1-1/4 cups all-purpose flour
1/2 tsp. baking powder
1/4 tsp. EACH baking soda and salt
1 cup toasted ground oats*
1 egg white, beaten slightly
coarse or granulated sugar

Beat butter and sugar together until creamy. Mix in egg, lemon extract, vanilla, lemon peel and sour cream. Beat until smooth. In a separate bowl, stir together flour, baking powder, soda and salt. Add to creamed mixture. Stir in oats. Chill thoroughly. Roll out dough on a floured board to 3/8-inch thickness. Cut into designs using cookie cutters or a pastry wheel. Place on a greased baking sheet. Brush with egg white and sprinkle with coarse sugar. Bake in a 375°F. oven for 10 minutes, or until golden brown. Remove to wire racks to cool. Makes 3-1/2 dozen.

Hint: If desired, shape dough into two rolls, each about 1-3/4 inches in diameter. Wrap in plastic wrap and chill. Slice thinly and bake as directed above.

*To make toasted and ground oats: Spread 1 cup rolled oats on an ungreased baking sheet. Place under broiler until lightly browned, turning occasionally. Cool. Grind in food processor or blender.

Pressed and Hand Shaped

These kinds of cookies demand tender loving care. Hand shaping or pressing takes awhile. However, once you get the routine down pat, it's amazing how quickly a rhythm and tempo can be established. Then the task goes quickly.

When you use your hands to shape the cookies, especially if the dough contains a lot of butter, wet your hands with cold water from time to time and the dough won't stick to your palms.

Chocolate Spritz

There are many shapes into which a Spritz cookie can be pressed. Some of the more popular ones are wreaths, Christmas trees, stars and bars which are the easiest. To make these, simply fit your cookie press with the small star tip (about 1/2-inch wide). This is the disc used to make wreaths. Press a continuous rope of dough, lengthwise onto your cookie sheet. Place ropes of dough about 2 inches apart. When the cookies are done, remove them from the oven and immediately cut them into 3-inch lengths, or bars. Frost these bars with a chocolate drizzle and top them off with chocolate sprinkles if you like. This version of chocolate Spritz will yeild as many as 2 dozen more cookies than pressing them in almost any other shape.

1 cup butter, at room temperature
1 cup sugar
1 egg PLUS 1 egg yolk
2 ozs. unsweetened chocolate, melted
1 tsp. vanilla
2-1/2 cups all purpose flour
1 tsp. baking powder

Chocolate Drizzle: (optional)
1 oz. unsweetened chocolate, melted
1-1/2 cups powdered sugar
1 tsp. vanilla
1/2 cup (or more) cream or milk
chocolate sprinkles

Beat butter and sugar together until creamy. Mix in egg, egg yolk, chocolate and vanilla. In a separate bowl, stir together flour and baking powder. Add to creamed mixture. Beat well. Spoon dough into cookie press until 3/4 full. Press any desired shape out onto ungreased cookie sheets. Bake in a 375°F. oven for 6 to 8 minutes, or until just set. Remove from oven and transfer immediately to wire racks to cool. While cookies are cooling, prepare Drizzle. Combine all Drizzle ingredients in a bowl and mix until smooth. Add enough cream or milk to make icing of drizzling consistency. Drizzle small amount over each cookie. Top each iced cookie with chocolate sprinkles, if desired. Makes 4 to 5 dozen cookies.

Hint: If unfrosted they will freeze well.

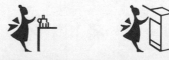

Chocolate Pfeffernuesse

3 eggs, at room temperature
1-1/2 cups sugar
2-1/2 cups all-purpose flour
3/4 tsp. cinnamon
1/2 tsp. cloves
1/4 tsp. EACH allspice,
    salt and black pepper

1/2 cup finely chopped almonds
2 ozs. semi-sweet chocolate, grated
3 tbs. finely chopped candied
    citron or orange peel (optional)
powdered sugar

112

In a large mixing bowl, beat eggs until foamy. Gradually add sugar and beat until thick and lemon-colored (about 10 minutes). In a separate bowl, stir together flour, cinnamon, cloves, allspice, salt and pepper. Add to egg mixture. Beat well. Add nuts, chocolate and candied fruit. Stir well. Cover and chill several hours or overnight. Dust hands lightly with flour and pinch off small pieces of dough, about 1-1/2 teaspoons each, and shape into balls. Arrange on well-greased baking sheets. Bake in a 350°F. oven for 20 minutes, or until lightly browned. Remove to wire racks and let cool slightly. Roll in powdered sugar while still warm. Makes about 5 dozen.

Chocolate Snaperoos

These chocolate nut rounds are wonderfully crispy. Filberts, almonds, pecans and walnuts all blend well with this flavor treat.

1/2 cup butter, at room temperature
1 cup sugar
1 egg
1/4 cup light or
   dark corn syrup
2 ozs. unsweetened
   baking chocolate, melted

2 cups all-purpose flour
1/2 tsp. baking soda
1/2 tsp. salt
2/3 cup finely chopped
   filberts or other nuts
granulated sugar

Beat butter and sugar together until creamy. Add egg, corn syrup and chocolate. Beat well. In a separate bowl, stir together flour, soda and salt. Add to creamed mixture. Beat well. Stir in nuts. Pinch off small pieces of dough and shape into 1-inch balls. Roll in granulated sugar. Place 3 inches apart on greased baking sheets. Dip the bottom of a glass in sugar and firmly flatten balls. Bake in a 350°F. oven for 12 to 15 minutes, or until set. Immediately remove to wire rack to cool. Makes about 3 dozen.

Chocolate Nut Crescents

This versatile dough can be handled in several ways. Instead of crescents, how about moons or half moons? For moons, prepare the dough as directed below. Shape it into a cylinder 1-1/2 inches wide. Wrap it in waxed paper and chill until firm. Slice the cylinder into 1/4-inch thick rounds. Bake as directed below, but shorten baking time by 2 to 3 minutes. For half moons, simply cut 1/4-inch thick rounds in half. Bake and, if you wish, dip half of the half moon into melted, semi-sweet chocolate. I like to roll the chocolate dipped end in finely chopped almonds too.

114

1 cup butter, at room temperature
2/3 cup sugar
1 egg yolk
1 tsp. vanilla

1/4 tsp. salt
2-1/3 cups all-purpose flour
1/4 cup unsweetened cocoa
3/4 cup finely chopped almonds or filberts

Beat butter and sugar together until creamy. Add egg yolk, vanilla and salt. Beat until light. In separate bowl, stir together flour and cocoa. Add to creamed mixture, beating until smoothly blended. Stir in nuts. Roll dough into ropes about 1/2-inch thick. Cut off 2-inch lengths and shape into crescents. Place on lightly greased baking sheets. Bake in a 350°F. oven for 8 to 10 minutes, or until set. Remove immediately from pan and let cool on wire racks. Makes 4-1/2 dozen.

Brandy Balls

This old-fashioned nut ball doesn't need baking. Bourbon or rum may substitute for brandy. It's a holiday favorite!

2-1/2 cups vanilla wafer cookie crumbs (about 60 wafers or one 7-1/4 oz. box)
1 cup sifted powdered sugar
2 tbs. unsweetened cocoa
1/4 cup brandy
1 cup finely chopped pecans or walnuts
3 tbs. light corn syrup
powdered sugar

Place cookie crumbs, sugar, cocoa, brandy, pecans and corn syrup in a mixing bowl. Mix until thoroughly combined. Shape into round balls, about 1 inch in diameter. Roll balls in powdered sugar. Store in an air-tight container for 1 day before serving. This will allow the flavors to mingle. Makes about 3-1/2 dozen.

Hint: If using a food processor, process vanilla wafers first. Then add remaining ingredients, using whole nuts. Process until mixture combines and nuts chop.

Chocolate Snowdrops

Sugared chocolate balls are teasing morsels. They are "Kissing Cousins" to Mexican wedding cakes.

1/2 cup butter, at room temperature
3 tbs. powdered sugar
2/3 cup all-purpose flour
1/3 cup unsweetened cocoa

3/4 cup finely chopped almonds
  (2/3 cup whole almonds)
2/3 cup sifted powdered sugar

Beat butter and the 3 tablespoons sugar together until creamy. In a separate bowl, stir together flour and cocoa. Add to creamed mixture. Beat well. Add nuts and mix well. Pat into a ball, wrap in plastic wrap, and chill 1 hour. Take rounded teaspoonfuls of dough and roll them into balls. Place 2 inches apart on greased baking sheets. Bake in a 350°F. oven for 20 minutes, or until firm and lightly browned underneath. Remove from oven and let cool on wire racks for 3 minutes. Roll in powdered sugar and let cool completely. Makes about 3 dozen.

Hint: If using a food processor, place butter, 3 tablespoons powdered sugar, flour, cocoa and whole almonds in work bowl. Process until blended about 30 seconds. Scrape down sides and process again until ball of dough forms, about 15 seconds.

Chocolate-Tipped Orange Sticks

1/2 cup butter, at room temperature
1/2 cup sugar
1 egg yolk
2 tbs. frozen orange juice concentrate, thawed and undiluted
2 tsp. grated orange peel
1-1/2 cups all-purpose flour
1/2 tsp. baking powder
4 ozs. semi-sweet chocolate, melted

118

Beat butter and sugar together until creamy. Mix in egg yolk, orange juice concentrate, and orange peel. In a separate bowl, stir together flour and baking powder. Add to creamed mixture. Beat well. Chill until firm. Roll small pieces of dough into pencil-like sticks and cut into 2-inch lengths. Place 2 inches apart on greased baking sheets. Bake in a 350°F. oven for 10 minutes, or until golden brown. Remove to wire racks and let cool. Frost half of each cookie with melted chocolate. Place on a foil lined pan and chill until set. Makes about 4 dozen cookies.

Filbert Kisses

This specialty from Peggy Allsworth's Oregon kitchen has been treasured for over 50 years. Now her great grandchildren are discovering them.

2-1/2 cups filberts
2 eggs, at room temperature
1 cup firmly packed light brown sugar
1 tsp. grated lemon peel

2 tbs. all-purpose flour
1/8 tsp. salt
granulated sugar

Grind the nuts in a blender or food processor or grate in a nut grater. Spread out in a shallow baking pan and bake in a 300°F. oven until lightly toasted, about 10 minutes. Let cool. Beat eggs with electric mixer or wire whisk until thick and pale in color, about 7 minutes. Gradually beat in brown sugar, 1 tablespoon at a time. Mix in lemon peel. In a separate bowl, stir together nuts, flour and salt. Add to egg mixture. Mix just until combined. Chill 1 hour. With a teaspoon, spoon out small balls of dough about 3/4-inch in diameter. Roll each in granulated sugar, coating evenly. Place on a greased baking sheet. Bake in a 325°F. oven for 12 minutes, or until lightly browned and still soft inside. Transfer to racks to cool. Makes about 2-1/2 dozen.

Chocolate Pistachio Sticks

Each cookie bar is frosted with chocolate and then pistachio coated, making an eye-catching sweet.

3/4 cup butter, at room temperature
3/4 cup firmly packed brown sugar
1-1/2 tsp. grated lemon peel
1-1/4 cups all-purpose flour
1/4 cup unsweetened cocoa
1 pkg. (6 ozs.) semi-sweet chocolate, melted
1/2 cup chopped pistachio nuts or pecans

Beat butter and sugar together until creamy. Beat in lemon peel. In a separate bowl, stir together flour and cocoa. Add to creamed mixture. Mix well. On a lightly floured board, roll dough into long ropes, 1/2-inch thick. Cut into 2-inch lengths. Place on greased baking sheets. Bake in a 325°F. oven for 15 minutes, or until set. Remove immediately to wire racks and let cool. Frost half of each cookie with melted chocolate and then roll chocolate coated half in chopped nuts. Makes about 2-1/2 dozen.

Cinnamon Nut Crisps

These thin spicy wafers are swiftly shaped by pressing out dough rounds with a glass dipped in granulated sugar.

1 cup butter, at room temperature
1 cup firmly packed brown sugar
2 tbs. sour cream
1 tsp. vanilla
2 cups all-purpose flour

1/4 tsp. baking soda
2 tsp. cinnamon
1/2 cup lightly toasted, chopped
    almonds, filberts, or walnuts

122

Beat butter and sugar together until creamy. Mix in sour cream and vanilla. In a separate bowl, stir together flour, baking soda and cinnamon. Add to creamed mixture, mixing until blended. Stir in toasted nuts. Chill 2 hours, or until firm. Drop rounded teaspoonfuls of dough onto ungreased baking sheet, placing each cookie 3 inches apart. Dip the base of a glass in granulated sugar. Press each cookie until thin. Bake in a 375°F. oven for 6 to 8 minutes, or until golden brown. Remove immediately to wire rack and let cool. Makes about 4 dozen.

Filbert Sand Dollars

Use a cookie stamp to emboss a design on these butter cookies. An antique glass with a raised "sand dollar" pattern is traditional in our home.

1 cup butter, at room temperature
1/2 cup sugar
1/2 tsp. vanilla
2 cups all-purpose flour
1/2 cup finely chopped filberts or almonds
granulated sugar

Beat butter and sugar together until creamy. Beat in vanilla. Add flour and almonds, mixing until smoothly blended. Pinch off small balls of dough, about the size of a large filbert. Roll each into a ball between the palms of the hands. Place on lightly greased baking sheet. Dip a cookie stamp or the base of a glass into a bowl of sugar. Press balls of dough to flatten, making a circle with cracked edges. Bake in a 325°F. oven for 20 to 25 minutes, or until golden brown. Makes about 2-1/2 dozen cookies.

Raspberry-Filled Thimbles

The combination of raspberries and filberts is a prize-winning one in these ambrosial cookie rounds. However, apricot and blueberry jam also make a luscious filling for these treats.

1/2 cup butter, at room temperature
1/4 cup firmly packed brown sugar
1 egg, separated
dash salt

1 cup all-purpose flour
3/4 cup very finely chopped filberts
raspberry jam

Beat butter and sugar together until creamy. Add egg yolk and salt. Mix well. Stir in flour and beat until smooth. Pinch off small balls of dough and roll between the palms of the hands to form balls the size of a filbert. Dip each ball in slightly beaten egg white. Roll in chopped nuts. Place 1 inch apart on a greased baking sheet. With the top of a finger, make a depression in the center of each cookie and fill with a small amount of jam (about 1/2 teaspoon). Bake in a 350°F. oven for 12 to 15 minutes, or until lightly browned. Makes 3 dozen.

Hint: A cork from a wine bottle makes the perfect tool for producing neat and uniform indentations in these cookies. Dip it in flour occasionally to keep it from sticking.

Mexican Wedding Cakes

This timeless cookie has a slight variation in almost every country. These buttery, rich little snowballs melt in your mouth. Mexican Wedding Cakes keep well for to 2 weeks, if covered tightly.

1/2 cup butter, at room temperature
1/4 cup powdered sugar
1 tsp. vanilla
1 cup all-purpose flour

1/8 tsp. salt
1 cup finely chopped pecans,
  filberts, or walnuts
powdered sugar for rolling

Beat butter and sugar together until creamy. Mix in vanilla. Add flour and salt. Beat until smooth. Stir in nuts. Shape into 1/2-inch balls. Place on ungreased baking sheet. Bake in a 350°F. oven for 15 minutes, or until lightly browned. Remove from oven and quickly roll the hot cookies in powdered sugar. Let cool and roll again in sugar. Makes about 3 dozen.

Hint: If using a food processor, place all ingredients, except powdered sugar for rolling, in processor. Add nuts whole, they will chop as they blend. Process until blended, about 30 seconds. Scrape down sides with spatula and process again until ball of dough forms, about 15 seconds.

Spicy Almond Crescents

Hard-cooked egg yolks produce a delicate texture for these cinnamon-coated German cookies.

1/2 cup butter, at room temperature
2/3 cup sugar
2 hard-cooked egg yolks, sieved
1 egg, separated
1/2 tsp. vanilla
1/4 tsp. almond extract
1-1/2 cups all-purpose flour
1/3 cup finely chopped
   blanched almonds
1/2 tsp. ground cinnamon

Beat butter and 1/3 cup of the sugar together until creamy. Beat in sieved egg yolks, raw egg yolk, vanilla and almond extracts. Mix in flour. Beat egg whites until foamy and set aside. Mix remaining 1/3 cup sugar with nuts and cinnamon and set

aside. To shape cookies, pinch off a walnut-sized ball of dough and roll it into a crescent, tapering the ends. Dip in beaten egg white and then in cinnamon-sugar. Place on greased baking sheets and bake in a 325°F. oven for 20 minutes, or until golden brown. Makes 2 dozen.

Hint: If using a food processor, chop nuts first. Remove from work bowl and proceed with creaming. No need to sieve hard-cooked yolks; simply add them whole.

Old-Fashioned Gingersnaps

While baking, these sugared balls flatten into rounds with a crackly surface, closely resembling the commercial variety. They are wonderfully spicy and crisp.

3/4 cup butter, at room temperature
1 cup sugar
1 egg
1/4 cup molasses
2 cups all-purpose flour
1 tsp. soda
1 tsp. EACH cinnamon, ground cloves, and ground ginger
granulated sugar for coating

Beat butter and sugar together until creamy. Beat in egg and molasses. In a separate bowl, stir together flour, soda, and spices. Add to creamed mixture and beat until smooth. Batter will be soft. Spoon out rounded teaspoonfuls of dough and roll into balls. Roll in sugar to coat lightly. Place on greased baking sheets 3 inches apart. Bake in a 325°F. oven for 10 to 12 minutes. Let cool on a rack. Makes 4 dozen.

Scotch Shortbread

A round of this buttery shortbread makes a welcome holiday gift. The dough also adapts to a cookie stamp if you prefer a special design.

1 cup butter, at room temperature
1/2 cup sugar
2-1/2 cups all-purpose flour

Beat butter and sugar together until creamy. Stir in flour, mixing until smooth. Chill until firm. Divide dough in half. Pat or roll out each half into a circle, about 7 inches in diameter. Place on ungreased baking sheets. Using a knife score each into 16 wedges. Bake in a 300°F. oven for 25 to 30 minutes, or until lightly browned. Let cool slightly, then remove from baking sheet. Cut into wedges. Makes 32 cookies.

129

Vanilla Crescents

Good Viennese cooks keep a jarful of vanilla sugar on hand, ready for confections such as these. Any cookie rolled in powdered sugar after baking can be rolled in vanilla sugar instead. It may take a little foresight to remember to prepare the vanilla sugar, but it's worth the effort. You can also make vanilla sugar with plain, granulated sugar too. Use this in cookie and cake batters.

2 cups all-purpose flour
1 cup butter, at room tempertaure
1/2 cup powdered sugar
1 cup grated or finely ground blanched almonds
Vanilla Sugar, see below

Place flour, butter and powdered sugar in a bowl. Mix until crumbly. Add almonds. Stir to distribute well. Pinch off small balls of dough about the size of a rounded teaspoon and shape each ball into a crescent with tapered ends. Place on ungreased baking sheets. Bake in a 350°F. oven for 10 to 12 minutes, or until straw colored. While still warm, roll in Vanilla Sugar. Makes about 5 dozen.

Vanilla Sugar

1 vanilla bean   1 lb. powdered sugar

Split vanilla bean lengthwise and cut into 1-inch lengths. Bury in a jar filled with powdered sugar. Let stand for 2 days minimum. Improves with age.

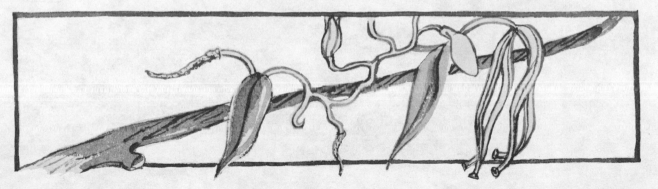

Holiday

The Christmas season ushers in cookies exclusive to the occasion. Beautifully sculptured Springerle, nut-laden Lebkuchen, Swedish Spritz and Viennese Marzipan Wafers fall into this category. These are the gems that shine for both gift giving and at-home parties.

There are countless attractive ways in which cookies can be packaged and given as gifts. Put them in metal tins, baskets, glass jars, cookie jars, clay pots or brightly colored boxes. Wrap them with aluminum foil, plastic wrap, Christmas wrapping paper or colored cellophane. Tie them with twine, yarn, ribbon, wire or strips of fabric. Use family photos, small Christmas cards, business cards, recipe cards or icing piped cookies for tags. Whatever combination you choose, just remember not to package different kinds of cookies together more than one day before you give them away. Cookies stored together for even a short time, tend to take on each other's flavors.

Christmas Butter Wreaths (Berliner Kranzer)

Sometimes this favorite Scandinavian cookie is adorned with candied cherry bits and chopped pistachios for extra holiday spirit. For variety twist strips of dough into pretzel shapes instead of rings.

1 cup butter, at room temperature
1/2 cup sugar
2 raw egg yolks
2 hard-cooked egg yolks, sieved
1/2 tsp. almond extract
2-1/2 cups all-purpose flour

Topping:
    1 egg white
    1 tbs. water
    1/2 cup finely chopped blanched almonds
    2 tbs. sugar

Beat butter and 1/2 cup sugar together until creamy. Stir in raw and hard-cooked egg yolks and almond extract. Add flour and mix until smoothly blended. Pinch off small balls of dough and roll each into a strip 4 inches long. Bring ends together, pinching to make a ring. Place on greased baking sheets. Beat egg white and water together until frothy and brush on cookies. Sprinkle with almonds and sugar. Bake in a 375°F. oven for 10 minutes, or until golden brown. Remove to wire racks immediately and let cool. Makes 2 dozen.

Hint: If using a food processor, there's no need to sieve hard-cooked egg yolks. Simply add them whole to batter.

Nurnberger Lebkuchen

In Central Europe this honey nut wafer is sandwiched with preserves or butter-cream and cut into diamonds or triangles.

3 eggs
1/2 cup firmly packed light brown sugar
1/4 cup honey
1-1/2 tsp. cinnamon
1/4 tsp. EACH cardamom, cloves, and nutmeg
1/2 tsp. grated lemon peel
2-1/4 cups mixed ground almonds and filberts
3 tsp. EACH finely chopped candied orange peel and citron

With electric mixer or wire whisk beat eggs until thick and lemon-colored. This will take about 5 minutes. Gradually add sugar, beating well. Beat in honey, cinnamon, cardamom, cloves and nutmeg. Stir in lemon peel, ground nuts, and candied fruit. Grease an 10 x 15-inch jelly roll pan. Line it with waxed paper. Grease and flour the paper. Pour in half the batter and spread it evenly with a spatula. Bake in a 300°F. oven for 25 to 30 minutes, or until golden brown. Remove from oven, turn upside down on a wire rack, and peel off paper. Let cool. Repeat with remaining batter. With a sharp knife, cut into 1-1/2 inch wide strips, then cut diagonally making diamonds. Dust with powdered sugar. Store in an air tight container with waxed paper between layers. Makes about 5 dozen.

Hint: Use a food processor to grind nuts. When processing, use 2 tablespoons of brown sugar (deducted from the half cup) with nuts. They will be more fluffy.

Apricot Brazil Nut Chews

Almost a pure fruit and nut confection, these are bound together with a caramel-like batter. They are one of the best cookies to ship at Christmastime. Yearly they arrive on our doorstep, sealed in two-pound coffee cans, without a crumble inside.

1-1/2 cups Brazil nuts, coarsely chopped
1 cup filberts or almonds, chopped
1/2 cup walnuts, chopped
8 ozs. whole pitted dates,
    chopped (about 1-1/4 cups)
1-1/4 cups dried apricots, chopped
2 slices candied pineapple,
    chopped (optional)

1-1/4 cups all-purpose flour
1/2 tsp. EACH baking soda,
    baking powder and cinnamon
1/4 tsp. salt
1/2 cup butter
3/4 cup firmly packed brown sugar
1 egg

Mix nuts and fruits with 1/4 cup of the flour and set aside. Sift remaining 1 cup flour with soda, baking powder, cinnamon and salt. Beat butter and brown sugar together until light and creamy. Beat in egg. Add dry ingredients, beating until smooth. Mix in fruit and nut mixture. Drop by rounded teaspoonfuls onto a greased baking sheet. Bake in a 350°F. oven for 10 to 12 minutes, or until lightly browned. Remove to wire racks to cool. *Makes about 6 dozen.*

Hint: It's best to hand chop the nuts and fruit in this recipe. They retain a more agreeable coarseness.

Paximadia

This Greek version of zwieback is traditionally a dunker served with richly brewed coffee. It is also a fine picnic cookie.

1/2 cup butter, at room temperature
2/3 cup sugar
2 eggs
1-1/2 tsp. crushed anise seed
1 tsp. grated orange peel
2 cups all-purpose flour
1 tsp. baking powder
1/2 tsp. salt
1/2 cup coarsely chopped almonds

Beat butter and sugar together until creamy. Add eggs. Beat until smooth. Stir in anise seed and orange peel. In a separate bowl, stir together flour, baking powder and salt. Add to creamed mixture, beating smooth. Mix in nuts. Turn out onto a lightly

140

floured board and shape into 2 slightly rounded loaves, each about 3 inches wide, and 3/4 inch high and 10 inches long. Place on lightly greased baking sheets. Bake in a 350°F. oven for 25 to 30 minutes, or until golden brown on the edges. Remove from oven and let cool 2 minutes. Slice each loaf into 1/2-inch thick slices. Lay, cut side down, on baking sheets and bake at 350°F. 10 minutes longer, or until golden brown. Remove immediately to wire racks to cool. Makes 2 dozen.

Kourabiedes

After they finish baking these Greek butter cookies are meant to be completely buried in powdered sugar, like a great snowfall. They are a lovable holiday cookie, that can be shaped into rounds, crescents, S's and cut-outs.

1 cup butter, at room temperature
2 tbs. powdered sugar
1 egg yolk
1/2 cup blanched almonds,
    ground and lightly toasted

1/2 tsp. almond extract
2 cups all-purpose flour
about 2 cups powdered sugar

Beat butter and 2 tablespoons powdered sugar together until creamy. Mix in egg yolk, almonds and almond extract. Stir in flour until blended. Pinch off pieces of dough and roll into 3/4-inch balls. Flatten slightly and place on greased baking sheet. Bake in 325°F. oven for 20 to 25 minutes, or until very lightly browned on the edges. Let cool until lukewarm. Cover bottom of shallow pan with waxed paper. Sift powdered sugar in 1/8-inch thick layer over waxed paper. Transfer cookies onto it. Sift more sugar over top of cookies. When cool, transfer to an airtight container. Makes about 2-1/2 dozen.

Chocolate Marzipan Wafers

1/3 cup butter, at room temperature
1/4 cup almond paste
1/3 cup sugar
1 egg yolk
1 cup all-purpose flour
6 ozs. semi-sweet chocolate
1 tbs. butter

Marzipan Filling:
1/2 cup almond paste
2 tbs. butter
1 cup powdered sugar
1 tsp. light corn syrup
1/4 tsp. almond extract

144

Beat the 1/3 cup butter and almond paste together until creamy. Beat in sugar and egg yolk. Mix in flour to make a smooth dough. On a lightly floured board, roll out dough to about 1/4-inch thickness. Cut out with a 1-1/2-inch wide cookie cutter, shaped like a star or a round one with scalloped edges. Place on a buttered baking sheet. Bake in a 350°F. oven for 10 minutes, or until lightly browned. Let cool. Prepare Marzipan Filling. Beat almond paste and butter together in small mixing bowl until smooth. Add remaining ingredients and beat until creamy. With a spatula, spread Marzipan Filling on bottom of wafers. Melt chocolate in the top of a double boiler over hot water. Stir in 1 tablespoon butter. Spread chocolate over marzipan layer. Makes 2 dozen wafers.

Macadamia Shortbread Stars

These sugar-dusted stars are a winsome addition to my holiday cookie tray.

1 cup butter, at room temperature
1/2 cup unsifted powdered sugar
1 tsp. vanilla extract
2 cups cake flour
1/2 tsp. baking powder

1/4 tsp. salt
1 cup finely chopped macadamia nuts
  or salted cashew nuts
powdered sugar for dusting

Beat butter and powdered sugar together until creamy. Add vanilla, beating until light and fluffy. Sift flour with baking powder and salt. Add to creamed mixture with nuts. Stir well. Cover and chill 1 hour. Roll out on a floured board about 1/4-inch thick. Cut cookies out with a small star or heart cutter. Place on ungreased baking sheets. Bake in a 350°F. oven for 15 minutes or until lightly browned. Remove immediately from baking sheets to wire racks. Let cool almost to room temperature. Then dust tops lightly with powdered sugar shaken through a sieve. Makes about 5 dozen.

Hint: If using a food processor, let 1-1/3 cups of whole macadamia nuts chop into batter as they blend.

Danish Roof-Tops

Almost pure marzipan, these triangular cookies are shaped like a golden roof dripping with frosting icicles. It is a favorite Danish holiday treat. It is one I discovered in Copenhagen at the Reinhard Van Hauen bakery on the Stroget. The Roof-Tops were lined up with the other marzipan sweets like a dress parade of toy soldiers.

8 ozs. almond paste
2/3 cup powdered sugar
1 egg white

Frosting:
2/3 cup powdered sugar
1 egg white

Beat together almond paste, powdered sugar and egg white until mixture is smooth. Pinch off pieces of dough about the size of a walnut. Roll each piece into a 2-inch long log. Arrange the logs on buttered baking sheets. Using your index fingers, pat the sides of the log to make a pyramid or roof-top shape. Bake in a 350°F. oven for 15 minutes, or until lightly colored on the edges. Remove at once to wire racks to cool. Prepare Frosting. Combine powdered sugar, egg white and 1 tablespoon hot water in a small mixing bowl. Beat well and add enough additional hot water to make frosting of pourable consistency. Drizzle over cookies in a zigzag pattern. Makes 18 cookies.

Swedish Almond Slices

These twice-baked cookies are perfect coffee dunkers.

1 cup butter, at room temperature
1 cup sugar
2 eggs
3 tbs. sour cream
1/2 tsp. almond extract

3 cups all-purpose flour
1 tsp. baking powder
1/4 tsp. baking soda
1/8 tsp. salt
2/3 cup slivered blanched almonds

147

Beat butter and sugar together until creamy. Add eggs, sour cream and almond extract. Beat until smooth. In a separate bowl, stir together flour, baking powder, soda and salt. Add to creamed mixture. Beat well. Mix in nuts. Turn out onto a greased baking sheet and pat into 3 strips, each about 2-1/2 inches wide and 1/2 inch high. Bake in a 350°F. oven for 25 to 30 minutes, or until golden brown. Remove from the oven and cut into 1/2 inch slices. Lay each slice flat on baking sheets and return to a 350°F. oven for 10 to 15 minues, or until lightly browned. Remove to wire racks to cool. Makes about 4 dozen.

Ancini

Italian biscotti come in many flavors. These have the licorice bite of anise seed.

1/2 cup butter, at room temperature
1 cup sugar
3 eggs
2 tsp. anise seed
3 cups all-purpose flour
1-1/2 tsp. baking powder
1/2 tsp. salt
3/4 cup coarsely chopped almonds or walnuts

Beat butter and sugar together until creamy. Add eggs, one at a time, beating well after each addition. Using a mortar and pestle, crush anise seed lightly. Add to creamed mixture. Mix well. In a separate bowl, stir together flour, baking powder and salt. Add to creamed mixture, beating until smooth. Mix in nuts. Turn out onto a lightly floured board and shape into two flat loaves each 1/2-inch thick, 2-1/2 inches wide, and as long as the baking sheets. Transfer to greased baking sheets. Bake in a 375°F. oven for 20 minutes, or until lightly browned. Remove from the oven and let cool 2 minutes. Then slice 1/2-inch thick. Lay slices, cut side down on baking sheets. Bake at 375°F. for 10 minutes longer, or until just golden brown. Remove to wire racks to cool. Makes about 4 dozen cookies.

Sesame Seed Shortbread (Koulourakia)

Twist these traditional Greek Easter cookies into pretzels or coils. They are an apropos accompainment to Turkish coffee.

1/2 cup butter, at room temperature
2/3 cup sugar
2 egg yolks
3 tbs. light cream
1 tsp. vanilla

2 cups all-purpose flour
1/4 tsp. cinnamon or nutmeg
1 tsp. baking powder
1 egg white
sesame seed

Beat butter and sugar together until creamy. Add egg yolks, cream and vanilla. Mix well. In a separate bowl, stir together flour, cinnamon and baking powder. Add to creamed mixture, mixing well. Cover and chill about 1 hour. To shape cookies, pinch off 3/4-inch balls of dough. Roll them on a lightly floured board, using the palms of your hands into 8-inch long strands. Twist each strand into a pretzel shape or fold strand in half and twist twice making a coiled strand (looks like a clothespin). Place on greased baking sheet and brush with lightly beaten egg white. Sprinkle with sesame seed. Bake in a 350°F. oven for 12 to 15 minutes. Makes 2-1/2 dozen.

Swedish Spritz

In Scandinavian homes, the buttery spritz is as integral to Christmas as the evergreen tree is to an American Christmas. And it is one that always stars on our holiday platter. Children delight in cranking out the dough with a cookie press.

1 cup butter, at room temperature
2/3 cup sugar
1 egg
1 tsp. vanilla
1/2 tsp. almond extract

2-1/2 cups all-purpose flour
1/2 tsp. baking powder
1/8 tsp. salt

151

Beat butter and sugar together until creamy. Mix in egg, vanilla and almond extract. In a separate bowl, stir together flour, baking powder and salt. Add to creamed mixture, mixing until smooth. Pack dough into a cookie tube press, using the thin flat wafer cut-out. Press out long strips of dough on greased baking sheets. Bake in a 350°F. oven for 8 to 10 minutes, or until edges of cookies are golden brown. Place cookie sheets on wire racks and with a sharp knife, cut diagonally across the strips making 2- 1/2-inch cookies. Makes about 5 dozen.

Hint: Use any cookie press plate design desired.

Springerle Cookies

There are countless wooden molds for this pressed German cookie. Among our family favorites are Saint Nicholas hauling a Christmas tree over his shoulder and a star-gazing Cinderella. This dough must dry overnight before baking.

2 eggs
1 cup sugar
2 cups all-purpose flour
1 tsp. baking powder
1/4 tsp. salt
1 tsp. grated lemon peel
2 tsp. anise seed

152

Using an electric beater or wire whisk, beat eggs until very thick and pale in color. Gradually add sugar, beating until completely dissolved. In a separate bowl, stir together flour, baking powder and salt. Beat into egg mixture. Stir in lemon peel. If necessary add a few more tablespoons of flour to make a stiff dough. Cover and chill several hours. On a lightly floured board, roll cookie dough 1/4-inch thick. Press

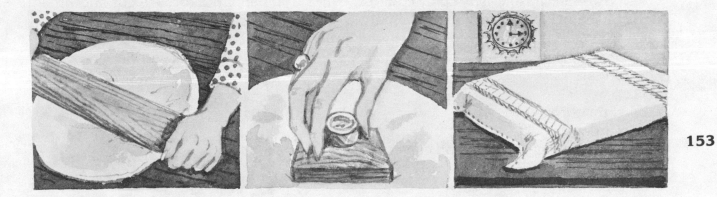

floured wooden molds into dough, bearing down firmly and evenly to leave clear-cut designs. With a floured knife, cut cookies apart. Place them on a greased baking sheet sprinkled with anise seed. Cover with tea towel and let stand at room temperature for 24 hours to set the design. Bake in a 350°F. oven for 15 minutes or until lightly browned on the edges. Transfer to wire racks and let cool. Makes 3 dozen.

Hint: If you prefer soft cookies, let the Springerle stand at room temperature several hours before storing them.

Christmas Gingersnaps

In Sweden these crispy spicy cookies, called Julepepparkakor, are cut out into all kinds of shapes: pigs, hearts, stars and little gingerbread men. They are passed to every guest who calls and also used to adorn the holiday tree.

1 cup sugar
1/3 cup water
1 tbs. light corn syrup
4 tsp. cinnamon
2 tsp. EACH ground ginger and cloves
1/2 cup butter
1-1/2 tsp. baking soda
1-1/2 tsp. lukewarm water
1 tsp. brandy
3 to 3-1/4 cups all-purpose flour

Mix sugar, water, corn syrup, cinnamon, ginger and cloves together in a saucepan. Heat mixture over medium-high heat stirring, until sugar is dissolved. Remove from heat and add butter. Let stand until mixture cools to room temperature, stirring to blend. Dissolve baking soda in water. Add to sugar-butter mixture. Add brandy. Stir well. Gradually mix in flour, adding enough to make a stiff dough. Knead well. Roll out dough between two sheets of plastic wrap until 1/8-inch thick. Peel off upper wrap and cut out hearts, stars and other designs. Bake on greased baking sheets in a 350°F. for 5 to 7 minutes, or until cookies are deep brown in color. When cool, decorate with powdered sugar frosting, if desired. Makes about 9 dozen.

155

Specialty

Certain cookies are so unique they demand a special category. These include the decorative and crispy wafers of Italian and Scandinavian origin that are baked in long-handled irons on top of the stove. They provide a delightful crunch to contrast with fresh, juicy fruit and ice cream. Rolled into cylinder or cone shapes, they can be filled with whipped cream and almost any fresh berry.

157

Chocolate-Tipped Orange Triangles

More a confection than a cookie, these chocolate-sealed candied orange slices are a delectable treat.

peel of 3 oranges (cut into quarters)   4 ozs. semi-sweet chocolate
1 cup EACH sugar and water

158

Place quartered orange peel in a saucepan. Cover with water, and bring to a boil. Simmer 1 minute, then pour off water. Cover again with water, bring to a boil. Simmer 1 minute; pour off water. Combine sugar and water in a saucepan. Bring to a boil. Scrape off most of the white pith from the orange peel. Cut peel into triangles, about 1 inch long and 1/2 inch across at base. Add orange triangles to syrup and let cook, uncovered, until the syrup is totally absorbed. Transfer to waxed paper and let dry. If still moist, sprinkle lightly with super-fine sugar. Meanwhile, melt chocolate over hot water. Using a small spatula, spread chocolate over tips of orange triangles, coating both sides. Lay on foil and let cool. When firm, store in an air-tight container. Makes about 4 to 5 dozen.

Coconut Date Fingers

This healthful snack is a wonderful fruity chew to tuck in a backpacker's or skier's pack. It also lends itself to countless variations with the addition of dried apricots, pears, or prunes and sunflower seeds or pistachio nuts.

2 cups chopped pitted dates
2-1/2 cups shredded coconut
1 tbs. orange juice concentrate, thawed and undiluted
1/3 cup chopped apricots, pears, or prunes (optional)
1 cup chopped pecans or walnuts
1 egg, beaten

Place dates, 1-1/2 cups of the coconut, orange concentrate, apricots and nuts in a mixing bowl. Stir to distribute evenly. Add egg and stir until blended. Shape dough into rolls about 1/2 inch thick and 2 inches long. Roll in remaining coconut. Place on a greased baking sheet. Bake in a 350°F. oven for 10 to 15 minutes, or until lightly browned. Makes 20.

Algerian Almond Diamonds

These cookie diamonds are perfumed with orange flower syrup. When you grind the almonds, add a little of the sugar, about 2 tablespoons. The almonds will be lighter and more fluffy this way.

1-1/4 lbs. (3-3/4 cups) blanched almonds
1 cup sugar
1 tbs. grated lemon peel
2 eggs
powdered sugar

160

Orange Flower Syrup:
   1/4 cup sugar
   1/4 cup water
   1-1/2 tsp. orange flower water*
   (optional)

Grind almonds finely in a food processor or blender. Turn out into a mixing bowl.

Add sugar and lemon peel. Mix thoroughly. Make a well in the center. Beat eggs just until blended. Pour over nuts. Mix well. Turn out onto a lightly floured board. Knead gently, 8 to 10 times. Divide dough into thirds. Shape into loaves, each about 1-1/4 inches wide and 1/4 inches thick. Cut diagonally into 1-inch wide slices. Transfer to ungreased baking sheets. Place 1 inch apart. Bake in a 350°F. oven for 15 minutes, or until golden brown on the edges. Remove immediately from oven and place on wire racks to cool. Prepare Orange Flower Syrup. Combine sugar and water in a saucepan. Place over medium heat. Heat and stir continuously until sugar is dissolved. Let cool. Add orange flower water and stir. Dip cookies into syrup. Dust with sifted powdered sugar. Let stand at room temperature until dry. Store in airtight container. Makes 4 dozen.

*Available in liquor or gourmet foods stores.

Florentines

With swirled chocolate coating its base, this delectable Italian cookie look professional. The candied orange peel is an essential ingredient to Florentines. Instructions on how to make it follows the cookie recipe.

1/2 cup sugar
1/3 cup whipping cream
1/3 cup honey
6 tbs. all-purpose flour

1-1/2 cups sliced almonds
1/3 cup finely chopped candied orange peel, see next page
4 ozs. semi-sweet chocolate

Combine sugar, cream and honey in a saucepan. Bring to a boil while stirring. Then boil gently without stirring until the temperature reaches 238°F. (soft ball stage) on a candy thermometer. Remove from heat. Using a wire whip, whisk in flour. Stir in almonds and orange peel. Drop by scant tablespoonfuls onto a foil-covered baking sheet. Bake in a 325°F. oven for 8 minutes, or until golden brown. Place baking sheet on a wire rack and let cool completely. Then peel foil from cookies. Meanwhile, melt chocolate in the top of a double boiler over hot water. With a spatula, preferably with a serrated edge, spread chocolate over the base of the cookies. Let stand until set, or refrigerate briefly to firm up. Store in a single layer in an airtight container. Makes 2 dozen.

Candied Orange Peel

3 oranges
1 cup sugar

Peel oranges. Cut peel into quarters. Place peel in a saucepan. Cover with water. Bring to a boil. Discard water and cover again with water. Bring to a boil and drain water again. Let orange peel cool slightly. Scrape off most of the white pith. Bring sugar and 1 cup water to a boil, stirring until sugar is dissolved. Add orange peel and simmer until liquid is completely absorbed. Place candied orange peel on a rack and let stand until dry. Store in airtight container.

Almond Wafers

It's easy to be smitten with these tantalizing almond rounds. One bite calls for another. Baking them on foil allows them to be removed from the cooking surface with ease. The foil peels off readily, even without prior buttering.

1/2 cup sugar
1/2 cup butter
2 tbs. heavy cream

2 tbs. all-purpose flour
1 cup finely chopped or sliced almonds

164

Place sugar, butter, cream and flour in a saucepan. Stir until blended. Heat over medium-high heat, stirring, until mixture comes to a boil. Let boil 1 minute, while stirring constantly. Remove from heat. Mix in nuts. Line baking sheets with foil. Drop rounded teaspoonfuls of dough onto foil, placing each 3 inches apart. Bake in a 350°F. oven for 6 to 8 minutes, or until golden brown. Makes 2 dozen cookies.

Hungarian Kiefles

These pastry crescents bake into thin flaky layers, sealing within the tart-sweet preserves and nuts.

2 cups all-purpose flour
1 cup cottage cheese
1 cup butter, chilled and cut into pieces
8 ozs. apricot jam
1/2 cup finely chopped walnuts or pecans
granuated sugar

Place flour in a mixing bowl. Add cheese and butter. Cut into pieces. Mix until the dough clings together in a ball. Wrap in waxed paper or plastic wrap. Chill several hours. Roll out 1/3 of the dough on a lightly floured board to 1/8-inch thickness. Cut circles 10 inches in diameter. Spread with jam and sprinkle with nuts. Cut into pie-shaped wedges, 3 inches wide at the base. Roll up from the wide end. Place on a greased baking sheet. Sprinkle with sugar. Bake in a 375°F. oven for 20 minutes, or until golden brown. Makes about 2 dozen.

Swedish Praline Crisps

On a Scandinavian sojourn, these scrumptious cookie wafers were sandwiched with cloudberry ice cream at the glorious Operakalleren in Stockholm.

2/3 cup unblanched filberts
1/3 cup all-purpose flour
1/4 tsp. salt

1/2 cup sugar
1/2 cup butter or margarine
2 tbs. heavy cream

Spread nuts in a shallow baking pan and bake in a 375°F. oven for 5 minutes, or until lightly browned. Remove from oven and let cool. Chop finely (a blender or food processor will make this easier). Place flour, salt, sugar, butter, cream and nuts in a small saucepan. Cook over low heat, stirring, until mixture starts to bubble, about 5 minutes. Remove from heat and stir for 30 seconds. Drop by rounded teaspoonfuls onto greased baking sheets, leaving about 4 inches between cookies to allow room for spreading. Bake in a 375°F. oven for 5 to 6 minutes, or until golden brown. Remove pan from oven and let cool 1 minute. Remove cookies from baking sheets, using a spatula. Immediately place each cookie over a wooden dowel and lightly press down the sides. Makes 2-1/2 dozen cookies.

Almond Paste Macaroons

These traditional macaroons exude a marvelous nut flavor and retain a moist chewiness after baking. They can be shaped in several designs and figure prominently in Polish and Russian cuisine, particularly on holiday occasions. They may be chocolate-tipped, nut-topped or filled with jam, too.

8 ozs. almond paste
1/2 cup EACH granulated sugar and unsifted powdered sugar
1/4 tsp. almond extract
2 egg whites

Place almond paste, sugars, almond extract and egg whites in a bowl. Mix with an electric mixer, or hands, until well blended. Spoon dough into a pastry bag with a large star tip, or pack it into a cookie press with a large star opening. Press out onto a foil or parchment-lined baking sheets making small rounds or wreaths. Bake in a 325°F. oven for 15 to 20 minutes, or until barely browned on the edges and set but still moist inside. Let cool on wire racks, then remove foil. Makes about 2 dozen cookies, each 2 inches in diameter.

Variation: try one of the following methods:

Crescent—By hand, press dough into 2-inch long crescents. Bake as directed above. When cool, dip ends into melted semi-sweet chocolate (about 6 ounces).

Fruit Rounds—After pressing dough into rounds make a small depression in the center of each. Bake as directed. Just before serving, spoon 1/2 teaspoon of apricot or raspberry jam into the center of each round.

Pinoccate—Pipe or press dough into 3 or 4-inch rounds. Sprinkle with pine nuts (7 to 12 per cookie). Bake in a 325°F. oven for 20 to 25 minutes or until set.

169

Lemon Tiles

This is one of many choice discoveries from a swing through the French country-side. These delicate little crisps go well with ice cream or fresh fruit.

1/4 cup butter, at room temperature
1/2 cup sugar
2 egg whites
1/4 cup cake flour
1/4 tsp. lemon extract
2 tsp. grated lemon peel
1/3 cup blanched almonds, finely ground
1/2 cup blanched slivered almonds (optional)

Cream butter and sugar together until light and fluffy. Add egg whites and beat until smooth. Add flour, extract and lemon peel, beating until blended. Stir in ground nuts. Drop batter by rounded half-teaspoonfuls (yes, this does sound like a small amount but it's correct) onto greased baking sheets, placing each at least 4 inches apart. Spread into 3-inch circles with the back of a spoon. Batter will appear thin and open in spots. If desired, sprinkle each cookie with a few slivered almonds. Bake in a 425°F. oven for 4 minutes, or until lightly browned. Remove from oven and **immediately** remove each cookie from baking sheet and drape over a wooden dowel or slender rolling pin. When cool, remove to a rack. Store in an air tight container. If left uncovered these cookies will become soggy. Makes 2 dozen.

Hint: If using a food processor, grind nuts first with 2 tablespoons of sugar deducted from the 1/2 cup. Remove from work bowl. Proceed with dough.

Pizzelle

This Italian word means small cake. Actually, these are thin, wafer-like cookies baked in a special pizzelle iron on the top of the stove. They are a familiar sight in Italian bakery shops, lined up in big glass containers alongside biscotti.

2 eggs
1/4 cup sugar
1/4 cup melted butter
1/2 tsp. vanilla
1 tsp. crushed anise seed
1 cup all-purpose flour

172

Beat eggs until light. Beat in sugar, butter, vanilla and anise seed. Stir in flour. Heat a pizzelle iron on a gas or electric stove until hot. Brush iron with butter. Add a spoonful of dough and bake 1 minute. Turn iron over and bake about 1 minute longer, or until golden brown. Remove cookie from iron and let cool on a rack. Makes about 12 cookies.

Molasses Brandy Snaps

These cookie cylinders are a perfect accompaniment to summer's fruits—juice-laden peaches, nectarines, apricots, and berries. They also contrast delectably to ice cream or a fresh fruit sherbet.

1/2 cup butter	1-1/2 tsp. ground ginger
1/2 cup sugar	1-1/2 tsp. brandy
1/3 cup light molasses	3/4 cup all-purpose flour

Combine butter, sugar, molasses and ginger in a saucepan. Place over medium heat. Stir until butter melts. Remove from heat. Gradually stir in brandy and flour. Drop by heaping teaspoonfuls onto a greased baking sheets, placing 3 inches apart to allow for spreading. Bake in a 325°F. oven for 8 minutes, or until golden brown and set through. Remove from oven and let stand 1 minute. Then, carefully remove each cookie from the pan. Shape it around the handle of a wooden spoon. Work quickly as they harden rapidly. Let cool, then store in an air-tight container. Makes about 2-1/2 dozen.

Scandinavian Krum Kager

These thin and crispy wafers are baked in a special decorative iron right on top of the burner of a gas or electric stove. They may be rolled into a cone or cylinder and filled with whipped cream, if desired. At Tivoli, the gala amusement park in Copenhagen, they are filled with soft ice cream, berry preserves, and a sprinkled flourish of praline or chocolate shavings.

1 cup whipping cream, unwhipped
1 cup sugar
4 eggs
1-1/4 cups all-purpose flour
1 tsp. grated lemon peel
   OR 1/2 tsp. almond extract and 2 tbs. toasted ground almonds
unsalted butter

Place cream in a mixing bowl and gradually beat in sugar, whipping just enough to blend it in. Beat eggs in a separate bowl until thick and light. Fold into cream mixture. Add flour and lemon peel. Stir well. Heat a krum kager iron on a burner until hot

through. Brush the surface with unsalted butter. Pour 1 tablespoon batter over iron. Bake until golden brown, about 1 to 2 minutes on each side. Lift cookie from the iron and immediately roll around a wooden spoon handle or shape into a cone. Let cool. Makes 32 cookies.

Dutch Caramel Cookies

Crystals of caramelized sugar provide these candy-like cookies with crunch. If you have a food processor or blender, let the caramelized sugar chop coarsely in one of these appliances.

Caramelized Sugar
2/3 cup sugar

1 cup butter, at room temperature
2/3 cup sugar
1 tsp. vanilla
1-2/3 cup all-purpose flour
3/4 tsp. baking powder
2 tbs. water

Prepare Caramelized Sugar first. Spread sugar evenly over bottom of a heavy frying pan. Place over moderate heat. Shake pan until sugar melts and caramelizes. (Watch it carefully, it burns easily. If it burns, the taste of the Caramelized Sugar will be bitter. Throw it out and start again.) Turn it out at once onto a foil-lined baking sheet. Let cool completely. When hard, remove from foil and chop coarsely by hand or with food processor blender. Set aside while you prepare dough. Beat butter and sugar together until creamy. Add vanilla. In a separate bowl, stir together flour and baking powder. Add alternately to creamed mixture with water. Stir in crushed Caramelized Sugar. Drop by rounded teaspoonfuls onto well greased baking sheets. Bake in a 325°F. oven for 12 minutes, or until lightly browned. Let cool 1 minutes, then place on racks to cool. Makes about 4 dozen.

Index

178

179

Hand Shaped and Pressed Cookies

Holiday Cookies

METRIC CONVERSION CHART

Liquid or Dry Measuring Cup (based on an 8 ounce cup)

1/4 cup = 60 ml
1/3 cup = 80 ml
1/2 cup = 125 ml
3/4 cup = 190 ml
1 cup = 250 ml
2 cups = 500 ml

Liquid or Dry Measuring Cup (based on a 10 ounce cup)

1/4 cup = 80 ml
1/3 cup = 100 ml
1/2 cup = 150 ml
3/4 cup = 230 ml
1 cup = 300 ml
2 cups = 600 ml

Liquid or Dry Teaspoon and Tablespoon

1/4 tsp. = 1.5 ml
1/2 tsp. = 3 ml
1 tsp. = 5 ml
3 tsp. = 1 tbs. = 15 ml

Temperatures

°F		°C
200	=	100
250	=	120
275	=	140
300	=	150
325	=	160
350	=	180
375	=	190
400	=	200
425	=	220
450	=	230
475	=	240
500	=	260
550	=	280

183

Pan Sizes (1 inch = 25 mm)

8-inch pan (round or square) = 200 mm x 200 mm
9-inch pan (round or square) = 225 mm x 225 mm
9 x 5 x 3-inch loaf pan = 225 mm x 125 mm x 75 mm
1/4 inch thickness = 5 mm
1/8 inch thickness = 2.5 mm

Pressure Cooker

100 Kpa = 15 pounds per square inch
70 Kpa = 10 pounds per square inch
35 Kpa = 5 pounds per square inch

Mass

1 ounce = 30 g
4 ounces = 1/4 pound = 125 g
8 ounces = 1/2 pound = 250 g
16 ounces = 1 pound = 500 g
2 pounds = 1 kg

Key (America uses an 8 ounce cup - Britain uses a 10 ounce cup)

ml = milliliter
l = liter
g = gram
K = Kilo (one thousand)
mm = millimeter
m = milli (a thousandth)
°F = degrees Fahrenheit

°C = degrees Celsius
tsp. = teaspoon
tbs. = tablespoon
Kpa = (pounds pressure per square inch)
This configuration is used for pressure cookers only.

Metric equivalents are rounded to conform to existing metric measuring utensils.